S0-BYX-648

# All About Psychoanalysis—
# In Questions and Answers

JOSEPH ROSNER

# ALL ABOUT PSYCHOANALYSIS

## In Questions and Answers

With an Introduction by
Herbert Holt, M.D., Past President of The Association
for Applied Psychoanalysis

*The Crowell-Collier Press*

First Edition 1962

Library of Congress Catalog Card Number: 62-17494

## Introduction

MAN'S EMOTIONAL PROBLEMS are as old as man himself, and Sigmund Freud was far from the first man to address himself to them.

We know from the ancient Greeks, for instance, that one of their number, the orator Antiphon, took it upon himself to do something about the emotional distress he noticed in those times. There were doctors who could tend to one's physical ailments, Antiphon observed, but there was no one to treat people's mental complaints.

So this man, according to at least one historian of the period, went down into the market place of Corinth and built himself a "kind of office." He advertised that he was now in the business of reducing men's mental anguish. When his patients came, he inquired into the causes of their distress, and he tried, by talking with them, to relieve their sense of suffering.

Antiphon may have had some other name for what he was doing—we do not even know how successful he was—but he was probably the first man that we know of to enter the formal practice of psychotherapy.

This historian notes that Antiphon gave up his work in this field after a time, because he felt he had more important things to do. Among these more important things, in his opinion, was making speeches, for which he was quite famous. These days, there are very few psychotherapists who have much time to make speeches.

In the more than two thousand years since Antiphon, other men have gone down into the market place in their own way and in their own time to try somehow to reduce the emotional distress of their fellows. They have used incantations, superstition, religion, medicines, something they called "common sense," and even instruments of torture. But it was not until Sigmund Freud unlocked the door to the human mind that psychotherapy really came of age.

In the narrow and less complicated world of the distant past, it was perfectly safe even for astronomers to believe that the earth was flat. In today's world, any such believers would be likely to have problems. So it is with the study of man. In the age of Freud, it is not possible to hold to the belief that the average man, if only he has enough self-control, can be master of his thoughts, his feelings and his actions. That innocent expression, "self-control," is itself a product of elements of which most men are completely unaware.

When one man looks at another, he tends to see a kind of total picture, minus the details. It is as if he were looking at a painting to which he responds with a single reaction: he likes it, he doesn't like it, or he is indifferent to it. An art critic responds in a more searching way to that same painting. To him it represents a combination of separate elements, and he analyzes them: color, composition, draftsmanship, even the special way in which the paint may be put on the canvas.

The average man is not too interested in the *why* of his reaction to another person. But the analyst, like an art critic, is very much interested in the details that go to make up the total picture. In fact, he is full of whys which do not occur to the untrained observer, the man who merely reacts but does not necessarily understand.

The human animal is a very complicated animal. He thinks, feels, hopes, fights, eats, laughs, dreams and suffers, among other things. He may go through a thousand and one different kinds of actions and sensations in the course of a single day. But despite all this, he tends to see himself as if he were a unified whole. It does not occur to him that he is an aggregate of details. It is the job of psychoanalysis, however, to examine those details.

To many people, psychoanalysis is only a word, and to some of them, perhaps, it is even an unpleasant word. There are few ideas in the history of human progress which have been so plagued by misinformation and misunderstanding.

It is obvious to anyone who has ever listened to people talking about psychoanalysis, that many men and women have questions about it. These questions can no doubt be answered in books already written, but far too many of these books have a built-in hazard for the layman. They are usually the work of professionals in the field, and because of this, they tend to juggle words and ideas which remain elusively beyond the average grasp.

The answers, then, exist, but for most people the search for these answers is hardly ever begun. And far too often, "the facts" about psychoanalysis are picked up by ear, or by people who "understand" them much too quickly. So the questions—and the misinformation—tend to remain.

This book is an attempt to answer many of those questions. It covers the Why, the What, and the How that seem to come most frequently to the layman's mind. And it explores not only some of the fundamental ideas of psychoanalysis, but also many of the more incidental but practical details as well. The reader will find here most of those questions which seem to be asked sooner or later by people who know a good bit less about psychoanalysis than they would like to know. He will also find the answers, written for the most part in simple, everyday language.

This work does not pretend to be a Bible of Freudian thought. It is not a manual, a textbook, or anything more than an aid to clarity in a field that needs as much light as it can get. In some areas where more sophisticated works dig deep, this one merely skims. Here and there, for good reason, this book may even omit. But on the whole, for the average reader, it may dispel many clouds and provide a needed measure of illumination. And perhaps it will encourage some to read other works that are more advanced in tone. And yet because of its clarity and simplicity, I think it can be used with profit as supplementary reading wherever courses in psychotherapy are offered.

Psychoanalysis is both a science and an art, and like any science or art, it has not closed any final door upon itself. Like geology or mathematics or music, it does not profess to know today everything that it will know tomorrow. But it has a great deal to offer in the field of human understanding, as of this moment.

It will be a good thing for psychoanalysis if those who have heard about it would, before they form an opinion of it, arm themselves with some facts as to what it is really all about. This book, in the form of questions and answers, is an attempt to help in that cause.

—HERBERT HOLT, M.D.

New York City

## Contents

# All About Psychoanalysis—
# In Questions and Answers

## Some First Facts

### What is psychoanalysis?

PSYCHOANALYSIS IS A COMPARATIVELY new and revolutionary branch of psychology. Its basic principles, which were discovered by Sigmund Freud, are not much older than this century. It is centered on the theory that there is far more to each of us than we are apt to be aware of.

The average person, for instance, likes to believe that he knows, most of the time, why he thinks, feels and acts as he does. Psychoanalysis holds that he knows no such thing. All the things we think, feel and do, it says, are largely dictated by a part of the mind over which we have little control. Psychoanalysis calls this governing element "the unconscious." (See page 33.) Despite its influence in our lives, most of us are completely ignorant of its existence as well as its power.

From the starting point of the theory of the unconscious, psychoanalysis tries to bring to light the real reasons why a person is as he is. Using the special techniques and theories developed by Freud and his successors, it tries to make the individual *consciously* aware of what had been previously *unconscious* to him. The result is self-knowledge.

Through this self-knowledge, psychoanalysts believe, a person may be relieved of a wide variety of mental and emotional problems. These problems have usually kept him from thinking, acting and feeling at the best possible level for himself.

### Who was Sigmund Freud?

Sigmund Freud was the founder of the psychoanalytic movement. Though no longer alive, he remains today its most important single figure.

He was born in 1856 in a small town in what was then the Austro-Hungarian Empire. When he was four years old, his family moved to Vienna, where Freud spent almost his entire life.

The family was not well off, but the boy was encouraged, nevertheless, in his desire for an education. He was drawn to medicine (he was to write much later) "by a sort of curiosity, which was, however, directed more toward human concerns than . . . human objects."

At medical school, Freud was particularly interested in the workings of the human brain and nervous system, and after graduation he specialized in this field. An early paper of his, incidentally, paved the way for the use of cocaine as a local anesthetic.

Freud's work in these early years won him a traveling scholarship for study in Paris and Berlin. At both these places he learned much about new developments in the treatment of emotional illness. He became attracted to the idea of treating hysterical patients by means of hypnosis.

Around 1895, with the help of another doctor, Freud began to develop the principles which form the foundation of psychoanalysis. Almost overnight, he became a controversial figure. His ideas, which appeared in a steady stream of scientific papers and books, were far too advanced for their time. As a result, Freud's contemporaries heaped upon him recurring waves of scorn and abuse. He had "disturbed the sleep of the world," but he believed so strongly in the truth of his ideas that he kept to his course.

In the beginning, Freud fought practically alone for what he believed, but with the years, more and more men rallied to his side. He died in London in 1939, after more than a year of exile from an Austria gone Nazi. By that time, he had seen himself accepted by much of the thinking world as the founder of a revolutionary method for achieving human understanding.

**How was the idea of psychoanalysis discovered?**

At the time when Freud began the practice of medicine, very little was known about the reasons for mental and nervous disorders. His post-graduate studies in Paris and Berlin had interested him in the possibilities of hypnosis as a tool in the treatment of such problems. But his results with this technique were at first not exceptional.

Early in his practice, however, Freud learned of a remarkable cure. It had been effected by a Dr. Josef Breuer, a general practitioner with whom Freud was acquainted. Breuer had been treating a young woman who had become ill after nursing her father through a long sickness. The girl had many symptoms, of which hysteria was one. Under hypnosis, she spoke freely to Breuer of the period in which she had nursed her father. As she talked, she drew a direct connection between each of her symptoms and some incident which had taken place during the nursing period. At the time of each of these incidents, it seemed, the girl had felt some strong emotion, which she had "repressed." (See page 54.) The hysteria, as well as other symptoms she later developed, appeared to be disguised expressions of this earlier distress.

With the information gained through hypnosis, Breuer was able to get the girl to re-live, consciously, the experiences which had produced the symptoms. Soon, her symptoms had disappeared.

This case is generally considered the first in which psychoanalytic methods were used. The effect on Freud, when he learned of it, was electric.

Freud began to use the Breuer technique with his own patients. His aim now was to explore the patient's past in order to uproot the hidden causes of nervous or emotional problems of the present.

In 1895, the two men published a book, *Studies in Hysteria*. In it, they traced the relationship between "forgotten" experiences and hysterical symptoms. They also indicated, on the basis of case histories from their own files, how the "bringing back" of such forgotten memories could result in the easing (or the outright disappearance) of a patient's symptoms. This was accomplished, they wrote, through discussion and through the release of the patient's pent-up emotional tensions—his hates, his fears, his most primitive desires.

In the Vienna of that day, the book created a great deal of controversy, most of it at the expense of the authors. Doctors considered the book interesting, even revolutionary, but generally unsound. Breuer was distressed by the storm which his work with Freud had aroused, and returned to general practice as a family physician.

But Freud now felt himself on the verge of profound discoveries. He sensed ahead of him an empire of research which medicine had so far barely noticed. With the departure of Breuer, he moved on alone, and he remained alone in his work for some years.

An idea of just how much alone he was in those early years may be gained from the following: In 1900, Freud published *The Interpretation of Dreams*. This book is a landmark in the history of psychoanalytic thought. In its first eight years before the public, the book sold only six hundred copies.

**What are the basic principles of Freudian psychoanalysis?**

Freudian psychoanalysis has advanced the following principles as the basis for understanding human attitudes and behavior:

I. Sex, in the broad Freudian interpretation (see page 39), is the single most powerful force in determining our feelings, thoughts and actions. This is true not only for the individual human being, but also for the society in which we live.

2. Sexual feelings (again in the broad meaning of that term) can be traced as far back as the cradle. They are present in the youngest infant. Anyone who has watched a baby at play has noticed the enjoyment it gets from its own body. An infant shows a great curiosity in picking up sensations through its mouth, its eyes, its hand, skin and, in fact, practically every part of itself.

3. Emotional problems are caused by the repressing influence which individual and group taboos bring to bear on our sexual feelings. Usually these taboos are first enforced on us by our parents—"Don't do that!"—while we are still in the nursery.

4. Even in the so-called average person there are elements of abnormality and a tendency to stray from the sexual norm.

5. Every person carries within himself a hidden reservoir of all his repressed sexual desires, memories and tendencies. This reservoir is in his unconscious mind.

6. Repressed sexual feelings fight their way to the surface of our lives in disguised, but socially acceptable forms. They do so in many ways. Dreams, myths, art, literature, slips of the tongue, clothing, and even jokes and wisecracks offer examples of this.

**How does analysis work?**

Psychoanalysis explores the basic mental life of the patient. It does this by turning a spotlight on his unconscious, a portion of his mind of which he knows little.

It seeks to interpret his dreams and random thoughts. It analyzes his current problems and shows how they are simply repetitions, in another form, of problems and situations in his faraway past.

The process is an intensive one, and usually takes a very long time. With the help of the analyst, the patient searches for the origins of his thoughts, feelings and actions. When his search is finished, he may then come to understand what really makes him tick. He learns to "know" himself.

A successful analysis helps a patient to lead a fuller life. It frees him of the harassing effects of problems he had imposed on himself in the past, but of which he is not *consciously* aware in the present.

**Is psychoanalysis concerned only with sex?**

No.

Because of the general lack of knowledge of what psychoanalysis actually represents, it is easy for many people to exaggerate the sexual element out of all proportion to its real importance in treatment. In many minds sex is a highly suggestive, even disturbing, idea. It often conveys an impression of secrecy, of immorality, and perhaps of shame.

Far from concentrating exclusively on sex, psychoanalysis examines the whole person. Among other things, it probes his search for power (or his fear of it); his yearning for prestige; his relationships with other people at home and at work; his feelings of hatred, whether open or disguised, of others or even of himself. It looks into these and many more of the elements that make up the mental processes of the average man or woman.

According to psychoanalysis, there is often some sexual root in these attitudes. But it should be remembered that here sex is not interpreted as the mere physical act of love alone. It is regarded as the sum total of all the individual's feelings of passion, affection and even friendship.

**Is it possible to analyze oneself?**

No.

We have only to look around among our friends and acquaintances to realize that some people are able to understand themselves better than others. But, according to psychoanalysts, it is not possible to do this really well without professional help.

Even with the guidance of an analyst, it usually takes a number of years before the patient understands himself fully. This is because the unconscious puts up a strong resistance to giving up its secrets. An analyst brings objectivity and professional training to bear on the patient's problems. Without this help, the average person cannot hope to achieve complete understanding of himself.

It is not unusual for people to feel that they understand themselves, or even that they have "analyzed" themselves. With many such people, this feeling serves as a convenient form of reassurance. It relieves them of the need to probe more deeply into themselves.

According to psychoanalysis, the person who tries to analyze himself is unable to make use of a basic prerequisite in the search for real self-understanding, the process of "transference." (See page 48). This is a primary tool of psychoanalysis. It is responsible for making the patient wish to please the analyst by trying to make progress. And it provides other important advantages as well.

Without transference, there can be no successful analysis. The individual who seeks the truth about himself, without professional help, is denied the benefits of this mechanism.

In the legal profession, there is the proverb that the lawyer who defends himself has a fool for a client. For very similar reasons, it might be safe to say that when someone professes to analyze himself, he usually has a quack for an analyst.

## Is psychoanalysis only a fad?

Psychoanalysis has been in existence for over half a century. The men and women who are authorized to practice it may do so only after years of rigorous study and training. (See page 77). It is no more a fad than surgery or the use of antibiotics.

Like other branches of medicine, this one is able to point to observable benefit in those who have come to it for help. And as is also true of other branches of medicine, it learns, year by year, a little more about its own possibilities for helping the patient.

**Does confession serve the same function as analysis?**

No.

There is a superficial similarity, but nothing more. In the course of confession, the individual is expected to tell what he knows. In the course of analysis, the patient is expected to tell much more than he knows. It is a fundamental belief of analysis that the basic facts about each of us lie below the surface of the conscious mind. The patient is himself not really aware of those facts until they are brought to light over an extended period of time.

Another difference: There is no clearly demonstrated proof that confession is able to rid a person of the direct symptoms of an illness. Psychoanalysis, on the other hand, can offer considerable evidence of its effectiveness in curing physical disabilities. Skin eruptions, asthma and ulcers, for instance, are ailments which are sometimes brought on by emotional difficulties. They are among the afflictions which psychoanalysis has been known to relieve.

**Is psychoanalysis a form of escape?**

No.

It takes a long period of study to make someone into an engineer, a pianist, or even a good boxer. Few people would call any of these pursuits a form of escape. Most of us are aware of the hardship necessary to achieve such goals.

Psychoanalysis, too, is hard work. Its training ground, however, is in the region of the emotions. And it rewards the patient with self-understanding only after sustained and conscious effort. In the course of it, a person must, for the first time in his life, examine the real reasons why he thinks, feels and acts as he does. Such self-examination, plus the necessary discipline of change, can be a painful process. In many respects, it is like an extended third degree, in which the patient plays the role not only of the "criminal," but also of the police.

**Should everyone be analyzed?**

No.

Many people, on their own, are able to make an excellent adjustment to the world in which they live. Psychoanalysis could do little for them that they have not already done for themselves.

For different reasons, there are great numbers of others who could probably get little help from analysis. Some are too old, for example, and others too firmly fixed in their ways of thinking and feeling to be able to profit from it. Additional barriers to treatment may be set up by religion, by certain influences of background, or even by personal prejudice.

If someone feels strongly—even for the wrong reasons—that analysis is not for him, then he is probably right to think so. A prerequisite for analysis is a measure of belief on the part of the patient that this particular kind of treatment may do him some good. Many people cannot be analyzed because they are unable to meet this initial requirement. Like religion, analysis demands some evidence of humility on the part of the newcomer if it is to be of real value to him.

Finally, there are men and women whose emotional structure was so badly damaged in childhood that the years have, in effect, given their problems a rock-like quality. For such people, psychoanalysis produces results only with the greatest difficulty.

**Why are childhood experiences important?**

Psychoanalysis considers early childhood to be the most important single period in the lifetime of every human being. What happens to us in the first five years of life, it holds, is decisive.

The experiences of those first five years live with us far beyond childhood, even though we do not ordinarily realize this. In the opinion of Freud, later events in one's lifetime, no matter how important they may seem to be, cannot erase the power of those early influences. Poet William Wordsworth had a somewhat similar idea when he wrote that "The child is father of the man."

In the first years of a child's life, it is particularly defenseless. It depends totally on the world around it for the satisfaction of its every need. And its needs are not only physical, but emotional as well. In these first years the child is also particularly self-centered. It "wants" continually, and it feels hurt by any denial of those wants. Unlike a reasonable adult, it makes no allowances for anything but its own "rights."

In this period, a child is likely to undergo a series of highly unsettling experiences which it is not completely able to accept.

*For example:* The child may feel hungry, but its hunger may go unnoticed for a time.

It may be cold, when it wishes to be warm.

It may want to be coddled, hugged and kissed, but this kind of attention is not provided. Or perhaps it is not provided often enough or amply enough to satisfy the child's wants. On the other hand, it is certainly possible that the child may be coddled too much.

It may have a brand new sister or brother with whom it suddenly has to share many attentions.

The child may make any of a large number of demands. The parent responds in one way or another to such demands, and sometimes even denies them. The way the child feels about such experiences, while the world is still new to it, is crucial.

The adult has no conscious recollection of these experiences of his first years. But despite this, they are not truly forgotten. They continue to exist as a powerful force in the unconscious. And without the individual's being aware of it, those experiences are able to assert this power in many ways.

The way the child has reacted to the early influences in his environment casts a special coloring on its later life. These reactions determine, for instance, whether he will grow up to be timid or aggressive (or evenly balanced between the two); frugal or generous; selfish or thoughtful of others; capable of loving or able only to resent, to doubt, and even to hate; believing or skeptical; gregarious and open, or solitary and closed.

Those experiences can also determine for him his political opinions, his choice of a profession, or even such a thing as his habits of personal cleanliness. They can, in fact, make themselves felt in almost every area in which he thinks, feels and acts. In a fundamental way, they shape how he feels about himself, as well as about his world and the people in it.

A man's choice of a girl to fall in love with may well be affected by these shadows from the past. The girl may be completely different from the ideal he dreamed about when young. He may even have a hard time trying to explain to his friends, or even to himself, exactly what he sees in her. But he is impelled to make this choice despite any such doubts. And when he has children, the way he responds to them will be largely determined by the responses he had to his own experiences as a child.

The events of his childhood, consciously forgotten, remain unconsciously present—and powerful. And "Only through psychoanalytic treatment," wrote Freud, "will he become aware of those events."

## The Language of Psychoanalysis—What It Means

### What is a normal person?

SIMPLY PUT, a normal person is one who is able to get along on good terms with himself, with others, and with life in general.

This is not as easy as it may seem. Life has a way of throwing each of us into circumstances that call for hard decisions. The normal person, however, is able to make his decisions with a minimum of hurt to himself and to others. He can meet hardship honestly, efficiently, and without feeling sorry for himself. And within the bounds of reason, he can accept the responsibilities of any position in which he may find himself.

Such a person can expect to live his life at its fullest possible potential, minus *unnecessary* worry or fear. He is able to show and feel his love fully (and he is able to accept love in return). And he is honest with himself as well as with others.

### What is a neurosis?

A neurosis—sometimes called a psychoneurosis—is an emotional illness which prevents a person from being really happy or efficient. The neurotic person is able, however, in all but extreme cases, to carry on his day-to-day activities.

Neurosis may show itself in many different ways.

*For example:* Fear of driving the family automobile.

Inability to get along with other people.

A tendency to have headaches while on the job.

A compulsion to count cracks in the sidewalk while walking.

The ways in which a neurosis can express itself are sometimes simple, sometimes complex. They can be hardly noticeable or they can be only too much so. But the ways are almost numberless.

Neurosis is an extremely common condition, although it usually goes unrecognized. Even a severely neurotic person may seem, to the uninitiated, merely "odd" or "eccentric." Although neurosis can cause a man or woman many difficulties, the person suffering from it is able, as a rule, to get along in the world as we know it.

**What is a psychosis?**

A psychosis is a mental illness which causes a person to lose touch with the world around him. A man or woman who is psychotic has a view of life, of people, or of himself, which is very distorted. Such a person has difficulty in working or carrying on day-to-day activities. He is likely to bring harm to himself or to others, or to get into some kind of trouble. He is a victim of what most people know as "insanity."

While a great deal is known about the effects of psychosis, very little is known about its causes. Recent discoveries have indicated a possible relationship between the chemistry of the body and some forms of psychosis.

**What causes a neurosis?**

Neurosis is probably to a considerable extent a by-product of civilization. Many primitive societies, with a minimum of taboos, show a minimum of neurosis. The more complicated a society becomes, the greater the number of things "one mustn't do." This increase in taboos brings about an increase in the prevalence of neurosis.

Every neurosis represents a war in the mind of the person who suffers from it. On the one hand, some instinct or desire in his unconscious mind demands satisfaction; on the other hand, some element there, related to the pressures of the outside world, says No! to this demand. The demand may be rejected for a variety of reasons: it may be immoral or extreme. Or it may in some other way conflict with social requirements. The demand, in any case, is "repressed." (See page 54).

Unable to assert itself in its true form, this demand then seeks out some weak point in the defenses of the individual. Here, disguised in a less objectionable form, it breaks through and enters his conscious life. The demand of the unconscious to express itself is thus satisfied by means of a sort of substitute. Unrecognizable for what it really is, it has now become more acceptable to the individual and to the world in which he lives. The way in which this substitute shows itself in his life is usually a symptom of the individual's neurosis.

*For example:* A child feels unloved by its mother. As a result, it feels resentment toward her, which it would like to express. (This is the demand.) But the child knows that ill-will toward one's mother is "bad," and these feelings are therefore smothered. (This is the No!) By the time it has grown up, however, the child, now a man, may have learned to detest all women in general. (This is the substitute.) A man who hates his own mother is likely to be condemned by the people who know him. But if he is merely a "woman-hater," he is likely to be viewed as, at worst, a crank.

## What is insecurity?

Insecurity is a word which is widely used to describe a kind of emotional distress signal which is even more widely felt. It is a form of deep-rooted unsureness about oneself. Its presence in a person may be hidden or obvious, and its effects may be continuous or infrequent. But most people have to live with it an entire lifetime.

This feeling first takes root, usually, in early life. A boy may feel deprived of the affection and understanding he thinks he deserves. Sometimes he feels unwanted, because his brothers and sisters seem to be getting much of the attention. He may even feel that his parents would have preferred a girl. His parents may not get along very well together, and the child may feel responsible for the friction he senses in the atmosphere. He may even feel, perhaps, that this ill will is directed at himself. Whatever the reason, he is made to feel inadequate, or even unworthy. This feeling, more than likely, will persist throughout his life.

There are many ways in which a human being may acquire a feeling of insecurity, which expresses itself in some degree in just about all of us. It plays a large part in making the average man think and act as he does.

*For example:* Because he is afraid that people may not like him, a man may be in the habit of always picking up the check when dining out with others. Or he may react to the very same fear by becoming an unyielding tightwad.

In one man, the feeling that he is inferior to others may make him a relative failure. He becomes frightened of any kind of competition. In another, the same feeling may result in an excessively competitive attitude. He may be the kind of person who turns the most casual situation into some kind of contest.

Insecurity is perhaps the most simple and yet most complex of all neurotic symptoms. It is a major target of the psychoanalyst.

**What is anxiety?**

Anxiety is a special kind of fear or worry.

It does not mean anything like the fear of lightning when one is caught outdoors in a rainstorm. Nor is it the uneasy feeling a man may get when he wonders if the beautiful girl who has surprisingly accepted his dinner invitation will really keep the date.

According to psychoanalysis, anxiety is any unpleasant emotional state in which the individual feels, consciously or unconsciously, that something fearful is certain to happen. In its own way, the feeling can often make him suffer as much as a physical ache or pain.

Our unconscious goals are usually hidden behind a smoke screen of other ideas or motives. For this reason, what a person really wants is not always very obvious to him.

*For example:* A man working at a job he hates may be forced to keep that job because he must support a wife and children. Unconsciously, he may resent his family, because his responsibility for their welfare forces him to do something he strongly dislikes. Consciously, he is an ethical person. He would not be able either to accept or to understand his deeper urge to punish his wife and children for putting this load on his shoulders. So he feels uncomfortable, worried, or generally out of sorts without really knowing why.

Although a man suffering from anxiety is not always aware of it in himself, he suffers the results of it nevertheless. It can make him feel unhappy, restless or insecure. His nights may be sleepless. He may be bothered with meaningless fears which waste his time and energy. It may be difficult for him to concentrate on anything. And he may feel all these pressures without really understanding the reason for them.

The poet Shelley includes in *Adonais* a few striking lines in this connection. They provide a reasonably good idea of what anxiety can do to the emotional life of a man.

*'Tis we, who lost in stormy visions, keep*
*With phantoms an unprofitable strife,*

*And in mad trance, strike with our spirit's knife*
*Invulnerable nothings.—*

Anxiety is a widespread neurotic symptom.

**What is the mind?**

Every one of us speaks on occasion of his "mind." When we do so, according to a good dictionary, there are likely to be any of half a dozen or more meanings we wish to convey with this word. We may, for example, be speaking of our opinion, our feelings, or our capacity to make sense. Or we may be using the word in some other way permissible in general conversation.

Like the conscience, the memory, or one's ability to play bridge, the mind cannot be pointed out on an anatomical chart. It is one of the most slippery and elusive terms in our language, and very hard to define to the satisfaction of everyone. Among psychologists (see page 78) there is very little agreement on what the word means.

When the psychoanalyst speaks of the "mind," he uses the word in the specialized sense implied by Sigmund Freud when he wrote that it "comprises processes of the nature of feeling, thinking and wishing." Freud of course included in his definition the idea that *unconscious* thinking and wishing were also a part of the mind's activity. (See below.)

For the purposes of psychoanalysis, the mind may be understood to be the total product which the brain can create in the form of emotions, symbols, processes and ideas. When we feel angry, when we dream, when we change our seat at a party to be more comfortable, it is the mind that is at work. Just as it works to make us decide our political opinions in one way or another.

The capacity of the mind to express itself, and the means it may choose to do so (consciously or unconsciously) are beyond measure.

It is the conscious that remembers the names of friends and acquaintances for us; it stores our attitudes on everything from the atom bomb to our preferences in foods; and it even makes us feel good when we think of those we love. It is what the average man usually means when he speaks of his "mind."

But the conscious represents only a tiny fraction of the total personality. Like the skin of a potato, it is obvious to us. But just as the skin merely hides the more important part of the potato, underneath the conscious lies the more important part of the mind.

### What is the conscious?

That part of our mental activity of which we are aware is called the "conscious." Unlike the brain or the heart, it cannot be described or located physically in the body. It is the one area of our personality which we always know about, and are able to control.

It is the part of us which keeps the facts of living straight for us. Like a giant filing system, it contains all the information, ideas and feelings of which we are aware. They are always at our disposal, waiting for us to bring them forward at the proper signal.

### What is the unconscious?

The belief that there is an unconscious part of the mind, and that it is vitally important in the lives of each of us, is the cornerstone of psychoanalysis. It accounts for the major difference between psychoanalysis and all theories of psychology that came before it.

In every one of us, the unconscious makes up by far the largest and most powerful part of the personality. It is a constantly humming powerhouse of mental processes, of which we are generally unaware. This crucial area of the human mind lacks a sense of time and of place, of right and of wrong. Like an unruly child, it knows only its own demands, and seeks to satisfy them, regardless of the cost.

The unconscious contains all the harsher memories of childhood which we think we have forgotten (but they are not really forgotten). Here, also, are our deeply felt secret hates and loves, the powerful but uncivilized passions and desires in each of us. Such feelings are too unpleasant (or even much too pleasant) to be approved or even recognized by the code under which most of us live.

These feelings are therefore repressed, tucked out of the way of conscious awareness. The average man does not realize that these unmoral ideas and wishes exist in him. He would probably resent the suggestion—if he did not laugh at it—should someone tell him about it.

In our waking hours, the repressed elements in the unconscious influence much of our lives. They affect the way we feel, think and act. At night, they express themselves in our dreams. The unconscious plays its part in determining the career we choose, the person we marry, the state of our health, and practically everything else about us that has to do with just living our lives.

It works a twenty-four-hour day, seven days a week, for an entire lifetime. And it is not possible for the average person to really understand this part of himself without specialized professional help.

According to psychoanalysis, the unconscious mind of each of us holds the secret of why we are what we are.

*For example:* In the average man, his conscious mind contains all the feelings and thoughts of which he is aware. This area might be represented by the United States. It has a history that we all know about, and its actions are usually expressed in its own name.

His unconscious, on the other hand, contains all the feelings and thoughts within himself of which he is not aware. This area might be represented by a foreign country about which the United States knows practically nothing, perhaps even doubting that it actually exists. Add to this the fact that this foreign country is able, through a highly efficient fifth column, to control to a large extent the laws, taxes, armed forces and general government of the United States.

In this image, the United States goes about its business thinking of itself as master in its own house. It does not suspect, even when things seem to be going wrong, that it is being manipulated by an underground enemy. The government operates, actually, under the dictates of a power which is interested in achieving only its own ends.

In just about this way, the unconscious portion of the mind dominates the personality of the average man and woman. Unknown, devious, but powerful, it manipulates both thoughts and feelings. This is true even though the way in which we think or feel about something may seem to us to originate in the conscious mind alone.

**What is the pleasure principle?**

An infant seeks constantly to gratify its every wish. Whether it wants the embrace of its mother, the removal of a tight diaper, or just something to eat, it knows how to make its need for attention known to those around it.

According to Freud, the unconscious mind operates in much the same way. Its driving aim is to satisfy itself. It seeks "pleasure." By this term, Freud did not mean pleasure in the limited sense of personal enjoyment. To him, the word covered any feeling of relief which comes from the easing of emotional pain or the reducing of tensions in the individual's unconscious.

The wishes and demands of the unconscious mind, like those of the infant, know nothing of laws, ethics or taboos. The do's and don't's of the world we live in are meaningless to it. It knows only what it wants. The goal may be love, or attention, or power, or something else. But always, like the infant, the unconscious tries to get what it wants.

Deep in the mind of every person, this drive sets up a constant demand for satisfaction. This is the "pleasure principle." According to Freud, it is the "sovereign tendency" obeyed by the unconscious mind.

### What is the reality principle?

All of life is a process of adjusting what we would like to do within the limits of what we are able to do.

The infant, calling constantly for every attention, learns in time that all its demands are not treated with equal consideration. The adult is kept by economics from buying that new suit of clothes. He is kept from going to Europe by his family responsibilities. He is barred from marrying the girl he wants because she will not have him, and the law (if nothing else) prevents his forcing his attentions upon her. These are ways in which conscious wishes may be denied by outer circumstances.

In the unconscious mind, the desires stimulated by the pleasure principle are held in check by an opposing power: Freud called it the "reality principle." It is the force in each of us which tries to govern the lawless demands of the unconscious. It tries to shape them to the requirements of the world around us, a world of laws and responsibilities.

The ideals of the reality principle are those of outward necessity, of law and order. Its relationship to the pleasure principle is like that of a firm parent to a willful child.

### What is the id?

Freud used *id,* the Latin word for "it," as the label for a particularly powerful force in the unconscious mind of every one of us. The id is a tremendous storehouse of energy, and it is entirely submerged in the unconscious. It is the source of all our passions, our instincts and our habits. And it strives continually to gratify them.

The drive of the id to achieve satisfaction in the life of the individual is often complicated. This is because it seeks to gratify its needs without any regard for morals or even logic. The id knows nothing of reality, as that word is commonly used. Its exclusive interest is the satisfaction of its own demands, no matter what the cost. It is completely dominated by the pleasure principle.

In attitude, the id might be compared with an especially obstreperous infant: it is entirely uncivilized, very demanding, and not the least bit interested in anything but its own needs and desires. There is a driving, untamed power about it, and it is not disposed to listen to reason.

The demands of the id are largely anti-social, and it hammers away constantly to make itself felt in the life of each of us. It plays a prominent role in influencing a person's life and character. But despite its importance in the average person's life, he is likely to be totally ignorant of either its presence or its power.

### What is the ego?

In ordinary conversation, when we speak of a person's ego, we refer to his vanity or sense of self-importance. When psychoanalysis mentions the ego, it is referring to something quite different.

The ego, like the id, is an extremely powerful factor in the personality of everyone. In contrast with the id, which is essentially lawless by nature, the ego is primarily a civilized product. It is a kind of control room in each of us which tries to keep us leading generally law-abiding lives.

It listens to the demands of our environment and sees that we try to conform to them. It acts as the agent, in the mind, of the world of reason and sanity. Like the id, it is self-centered, but it is much more realistic. The ego, in effect, can tell the difference between right and wrong, while the id cannot.

The ego is partly conscious and partly unconscious. Consciously, for instance, it tries to make us moral persons: The married man who is attracted to his secretary may never let her know his feelings for her. Unconsciously, the ego represses certain aspects of our character which it regards as immoral: The man who is attracted to his sister-in-law may be completely unaware of this attraction; through the pressures of his ego, he may be convinced that he actually detests the woman.

The ego works in each of us even while we are asleep. When our more unpleasant thoughts assert themselves in a dream, it is the ego which censors them. It forces these perhaps threatening ideas to appear in disguise. They show themselves in the dream in the form of symbols.

In every person, the lawless desires of the id clash head-on with the moral sense of the ego. As a result, the two forces are continuously engaged in a kind of invisible tug of war with each other.

They are like an older and a younger brother who have completely different ideas as to how the family business should be run. The older brother (the ego) knows all about business procedure and is inclined to be conservative. The younger brother (the id) tends to be daring, rash, throwing ordinary caution out the window. He is willing to risk everything on the most casual impulse. The older brother has his hands full trying to keep the younger brother under control.

There are times when the ego relaxes this control, and the id is permitted to have its own way. When this happens, the ego usually learns to regret it.

*For example:* In a fit of anger, a man might punch someone (and the consequences could be anything from being punched in return, to a lawsuit).

He might get excessively drunk at the office party (and the consequences could be a depressing loss of esteem).

He might pursue an attractive girl he strongly suspected was "no good' for him (and the consequence could be that she was in fact no good for him).

In Freud's own image, the id produces the driving power, while the ego handles the steering wheel in order to reach a desired goal.

Basically, the ego acts as an intermediary, or compromiser, between the impractical demands of the id and the practical demands of our environment.

**What is the superego?**

A person's superego is roughly identical with what we normally call his conscience. In his mental life, it represents the combined force of all the do's and don'ts picked up during his lifetime. These have become part of him through contacts with his parents, his teachers, religious influences, and other forms of moral authority.

The superego is largely unconscious in the personality. It is the mechanism which tells each of us what is morally right and what is morally wrong. Acting as a sort of overseer, or monitor, it tries to direct the ego along the path of what is right. It also has the power to punish the ego for yielding to the more reckless demands of the id. When we have done wrong, for instance, we tend to feel guilty. This is the punishment that most of us know as "the pangs of conscience."

**What is the libido?**

By Freud's own definition, the libido is "the energy . . . of those instincts which have to do with all that may be comprised under the word 'love.' "

But Freud's definition, still in his own words, "goes lower and also higher than the popular sense of the word. . . ." The libido includes many different kinds of love. It embraces the instinct for sexual love, for love of one's self, love of one's parents, children, friends, and even for humanity in general. It also includes love of inanimate objects such as works of art. And the libido is involved, too, in one's love of country, or even devotion to an abstract idea.

Freud maintained that all the separate kinds of love spring from a common source in the character of the individual. It was this source of psychic energy to which he gave the name "libido."

He noted, among other characteristics, that it is present in each of us from early childhood. And in each of us, the emphasis which this stream of energy places on any particular form of love is constantly changing. For example, during a single lifetime one person may center his love first on his parents, then on a pet dog, then on his wife, later on his children, and later still, perhaps, on a collection of paintings or on his religion.

### What is a complex?

A complex is a kind of emotional problem, and it is an especially complicated one. The word is used to describe a group of feelings and ideas, all related to each other, which stem from some central wound in the individual's emotional experience.

This is how it comes about: Something that happened to a man far back in his past has affected him deeply. The hurt has been so great that this man has repressed it. He has buried it in his unconscious mind. Like dirt that has been swept under a carpet, he may not be conscious that it is there, but it remains in his mind nevertheless.

Ordinary dirt may be innocent enough, but an injury of this sort, when repressed, is more like a piece of radioactive metal. This kind of metal usually appears to be harmless. But it discharges a kind of energy which affects everything around it. The original emotional wound, hidden in the unconscious, acts in much the same way.

Buried in his mind, this deep hurt of the past is able to fix itself on a particular pattern of ideas in the man's consciousness. These ideas become charged with waves of emotional electricity, and tend to influence his thoughts, his feelings and, in fact, his life.

Consciously, a man with a complex rarely understands the full extent to which his mind is at the mercy of these emotion-tinged ideas. To himself, or even to others, he may try to explain his odd behavior, his queer thoughts, with reasons which *seem* more logical than they actually are.

The Oedipus complex is perhaps the classic example of this type of problem.

### What is the Oedipus complex?

According to ancient Greek legend, it had been prophesied that Oedipus, newborn son of a king, would one day kill his father and marry his mother. Frightened by the prophecy, the king put the infant on a mountainside to die. A wandering shepherd found the baby, however, and gave it to a couple in another country to raise as their own.

The boy grew to manhood without knowing the identity of his real parents. Years later, after many heroic exploits, he won the Queen of Thebes in marriage. Some time after, a terrible plague fell upon Thebes. It was then revealed to Oedipus that a traveler he had killed long before, in a quarrel on a lonely road, was his own father. Also revealed was the fact that the woman with whom he now shared his throne was his mother. The prophecy had been fulfilled. In his shame, Oedipus blinded himself and left Thebes to become a wanderer.

This is the story of Oedipus in simple outline, and in

just as simple outline, according to Freud, it is the basic story of every neurosis.

Every child, because of the circumstances of infancy and early childhood, unconsciously yearns to gratify its sexual desires with the parent of the opposite sex. And, correspondingly, it resents its parent of the same sex. Among primitive as well as civilized peoples, however, there is a strong taboo against incest, and each of us becomes aware of this taboo very early in life. As a result, these dark feelings, though they are carried with us through adult life, remain buried deep in the unconscious.

The average person will go through an entire lifetime without realizing that such feelings exist in him. His conscious mind has carefully insulated itself against recognizing these feelings, because to do so would be too great a blow to the average person's sense of what is proper. It is for this reason that when these feelings express themselves, they are forced to do so in disguised form.

With most of us, the fear of "what people will think" causes these socially unacceptable feelings to be locked away deep in the unconscious. There, they struggle constantly to break loose from the jailer that keeps them penned in. This jailer represents our fear of "consequences." It is this struggle between something that we want, and something that we do not want, that breeds neurosis.

Sometimes these repressed feelings of the Oedipus complex are able to slip away from the unconscious. When this happens, they appear in our conscious life in some counterfeit form which is less obviously objectionable to us.

In its disguised form, the Oedipus complex expresses itself all around us. It does this not only by influencing the way a man (or woman) may live his life, but it expresses itself also in art, in popular music, in literature, in our humor, our profanity and in many other forms.

An example which is not too uncommon is the man who marries a woman many years older than himself. More dramatic is the occasional newspaper story that a girl has, for some reason, murdered her mother. Very often, these feelings show themselves in the individual in a fear of getting married, or conversely, in a tendency to marry (and divorce) too often. These are only a few of the many examples with which the world provides us. The stronger the Oedipus complex, however, the more obviously will this basic cause of neurosis reveal itself for what it is—a sign of emotional ill health.

Those who have progressed farthest toward an understanding of this problem in themselves, by whatever means, are usually closest to being emotionally healthy men and women.

Like other elements in the theory of psychoanalysis, the Oedipus complex implies the existence of highly uncivilized feelings in even the so-called "average" man. For most people, the idea that such feelings may exist in them represents an affront to their moral background. Such feelings are difficult for many to accept. The horror of even the suggestion of incest is very strong. For this reason, the theory of the Oedipus complex can be a personally threatening one to many people. And for some of these, it may serve as a plausible excuse for rejecting practically everything having to do with psychoanalysis.

**What is the castration complex?**

The castration complex is closely related to the Oedipus complex. It is a group or "complex" of thoughts and feelings focused on the individual's unconscious fear that he will somehow be deprived of his sex organs.

This fear is something more than the conventional awareness that one may lose an eye or a limb in some unforeseen accident. It is a deeply felt and specific dread, centered on one's sex organs alone. Each of us tends to say in jest what he hesitates to say more directly, and unguarded humor often reveals how widespread is the image of castration.

This fear is a common one among neurotics. Psychoanalysts believe that it may be found, as well, among those who are considered to be normal. But in normal people it is likely to be present with a lesser degree of intensity.

The castration complex is usually the result of longstanding fears that we will be punished for having forbidden erotic desires.

*For example:* A parent warns a child, in a particularly graphic manner, about the punishment the child may expect for masturbation. The warning feeds on the child's imagination and sense of defenselessness. As a result, the turmoil of feelings leaves an impression on the child's unconscious which remains there well into adult life.

Again, a child's sexual feelings for its own mother must be smothered when it learns that such feelings are considered to be "bad." The child's unconscious fear that he will be found out, and punished, can be another push in the direction of a castration complex.

This complex takes root early in life, at a time when a child's discovery of his own sex organs makes them seem all-important to him. It has a tremendous influence on the later development of the character and sexual attitudes of the individual.

It is often this kind of feeling which lurks in the personality of the man who takes a derogatory attitude toward women. Such a man tends to fear the female. He sees her as the eternal temptress who may lure him into the path of a terrible punishment. The result is contempt (or even hatred) of women. It is the reason why many men adapt themselves to lives of total sexlessness, or even homosexuality. It is also the reason why many men have difficulties in marriage.

A woman, too, may suffer from a castration complex. A girl learns, before she is very long in the world, that her body is markedly different from a boy's. This provokes in her a strong unconscious reaction. She feels cheated. It is as though, through no fault of her own, an important part of her body had been stolen from her. She may blame her mother for having brought her into the world in this condition, and this may pave the way to a lifetime of friction between them. And the girl's sense of personal loss may persist throughout her entire life.

When a woman has such feelings, she tends to see the female as having a second-class status in our society. To her, it is distasteful to have to play the role of a woman. Her attitude toward men, toward life, and toward herself may be strongly colored by the intensity of her feelings of "castration."

## What is the life instinct?

According to a theory developed by Freud in his later years, there are, fundamentally, just two basic instincts, or drives, in every human being. He called one of these the life instinct, and to the other he gave the name death instinct. (See below.) These two drives are completely opposed to each other in their aims and desires.

The life instinct, to which Freud gave the additional name of "the Eros" (after the Greek god of love), is directly involved with the libido. (See page 39.) It is a creative and affirmative force in every one of us. It comprises all our desires for self-gratification as well as self-preservation.

As its name implies, this instinct is a source of strength for the individual. It is firmly on the side of life, and everything that word might stand for.

Often enough, we read of some particularly heroic feat of endurance against seemingly hopeless odds: How some men have wandered half-crazed in a desert for weeks, till rescued; how others, starved and without water, have survived for more than a month on rafts in mid-Pacific; how still others have been subjected to extended and systematic torture and come through alive. All these are dramatic examples of the life instinct at work. But it expresses itself in less obvious ways as well: In our pleasures, our ambitions, our family feelings, love, in our capacity for optimism, and in other aspects of our lives.

**What is the death instinct?**

The theory of the death instinct, as advanced by Freud, is a particularly difficult one for most people to accept, or even to understand. According to this theory, there is in each of us an instinctive drive toward destructiveness and aggressiveness, and in each of us this tendency is directed primarily against ourselves.

Opposed to this drive is the so-called life instinct, which is primarily aimed at self-preservation and self-gratification. In contrast to the destructive death instinct, the life instinct is a force which is essentially creative.

According to Freud, the death instinct tries to steer the individual in the direction of death because only there can real peace be found. It is only in death, the final rest, that one can expect to achieve complete release from tension or from striving.

This urge to self-destruction (still according to Freud) is blunted or turned aside by the pressures of the life instinct. Sometimes, of course, the latter may fail at this. When this happens, the death instinct may assert itself nakedly in the form of suicide.

In the course of the speech that begins "To be, or not to be . . ." Shakespeare's Hamlet offers a good many of the reasons why death can seem attractive to a human being. He also offers some of the reasons why it may not be so attractive after all. Implicit in the reasons which Hamlet offers for *not* seeking death is the fundamental human instinct to hang on to life, and to preserve it.

The life instinct forces the death instinct to disguise itself in a variety of forms.

*For example:* As already noted, the wish to destroy oneself can be so overwhelming as to cause a man to commit suicide. If it were not quite so overwhelming, and could be influenced by the life instinct, this same person might simply become a masochist, one who enjoys his own pain. He might even invert the direction of all this destructive energy; he might turn it outside himself and become aggressive, sadistic, and perhaps even a killer.

Another man, under the same pressures, may turn to alcohol, or drug addiction. Or he may become one of those people who seem to have a special talent for being involved in accidents. Even someone who just doesn't seem to be able to hold onto a job may be expressing in subtle form the pressures of the drive to self-destruction. And one widespread and seemingly innocent expression of these feelings is the habit of biting one's nails.

The average man or woman is willing to accept the fact that death can seem attractive in certain types of circumstances: If one is suffering from some painful and incurable disease, for instance. It is hard to convince this same average man or woman, however, that death may be attractive (even if not obviously so) to people in less exceptional circumstances. But there have been men who commented on this very fact—the fascination of death—long before Freud dreamed of the death instinct.

For example:

SHAKESPEARE:

> The stroke of death is as a lover's pinch,
> Which hurts, and is desir'd.
>
> (*Antony and Cleopatra,* 1607)

JOHN KEATS:

I have been half in love
With easeful Death . . .
(*Ode to a Nightingale,* 1819)

MARK TWAIN:

Whoever has lived long enough to find out what life is knows how deep a debt of gratitude we owe to Adam, the first great benefactor of our race. He brought death into the world.
(*Pudd'nhead Wilson's Calendar,* 1894)

Most psychoanalysts of today make little reference to the death instinct as such. But they tend to accept most of the implications of this theory under the heading of man's instinctive drive to be destructive and aggressive.

**What is transference?**

Transference is a major tool used by the analyst to help the patient gain real understanding of himself. It is a mechanism of high importance in psychoanalysis, and without it no analysis is likely to be successful.

Each of us, at different moments in his life, has feelings about some other person which are out of proportion to what that other person deserves. The feeling may be one of love or of hate, of warmth or of disgust, to mention some possibilities. At such times, it is possible to have a combination of highly dissimilar feelings for this other person. It is not unusual, for instance, for a man to experience a strong sense of dislike and at the same time affection for some other man or woman. Usually when we have such mixed feelings, we do not bother to explain them either to ourselves or to others. And if we ever do explain them, our reasons turn out to be superficial at best. They are less logical than they may appear to be.

In such situations, a man is re-living, in relation to someone in his present life, the feelings he experienced toward some other person far back in his past. Something in the present person touches off a spark of unconscious memory. And when that happens, our relations with him (or her) become flooded with the feelings of the past.

These feelings of bygone days are summoned up against our will to do duty in the present. Most often they are feelings we originally felt toward our own father or mother. At that time, however, we did not express them because for some reason that would have been "wrong." We therefore repressed them inside ourselves.

In the course of treatment, the analyst serves as the perfect sounding board for all such repressed feelings. In the privacy of professional surroundings, the patient comes to realize, unconsciously, that nothing he is likely to say or feel will be considered in any way shameful or evil. The attitude of the analyst is expressed in the remark of the Roman playwright Terence: "I am a man, and nothing human is foreign to me." The atmosphere in the room is therefore permissive. And as time goes on, the patient feels himself more and more free to relieve himself of his real feelings.

As these real thoughts and feelings come to the surface of the mind, the patient is performing more than an act of memory. He is, in effect, re-living his past. He "transfers" it to the present. Without recognizing what he is doing, he brings into the room all the reactions to other members of his family which he felt in the days of his childhood.

He directs this confusion of loves and hates, likes and dislikes, fears, joys and suspicions, at the analyst. The patient now comes to see the analyst in a very special way. He has become the living symbol of all the people to whom the patient, in his early years, had an emotional reaction. These feelings, once scattered in several directions, are now concentrated and "transferred" onto the analyst.

This is what is meant by transference, and it may last through many months of the analysis.

But while the patient thus feels strongly emotional about the analyst, the analyst remains unemotional and objective. It is this objectivity, plus his professional background and experience, which enables the analyst to guide the patient out of the storm of his deepest feelings. The significance of these feelings is explored and interpreted. In the course of many such interpretations, the patient acquires a clearer understanding of the reasons for the way he thinks, feels and behaves.

## What is free association?

Most of us have had experience with a slip of the tongue; we have somehow, against our wish, blurted out a remark we would have preferred to keep to ourselves. Such happenings are simple examples, in everyone's life, of the principle of free association.

Our real feelings and thoughts about particular people, situations and things, lie hidden beneath the surface of our minds. Like germs in one's blood stream, these feelings may be out of sight, but they are still, so to speak, in one's system. They find ways to make themselves known to us, and the slip of the tongue is one of those ways. The repressed feeling has been enabled to express itself by "associating" itself with some conscious and more acceptable idea.

In everyday life, incidents of free association serve no constructive purpose, and there are occasions, of course, in which they may produce situations which are extremely embarrassing. But no matter how striking the example may be, the average person rarely recognizes the unconscious motive behind it. In the course of analysis, however, free association serves as a useful tool for digging into the unconscious mind.

In the analysis, the patient simply talks. He may speak

of anything that comes into his mind, no matter how bold, no matter how ridiculous. He makes no conscious effort to guide his thoughts, but lets them flow at random. In this way, rambling on, he is able to "associate freely" from one remark to the next.

In such moments, his unconscious feelings tend to assert themselves and give direction to his thoughts. The particular remarks he makes during periods of free association will usually give the analyst significant clues to the patient's underlying problems.

**What is a symptom?**

A symptom is a signal flag displayed by the body or the mind to indicate some form of inner distress.

Headache, sore throat and eye trouble, individually, may be just what they seem to be, and may be easily cured. The family doctor can sometimes recognize in each of these, however, the sign of some deeper ailment. In special cases they may be symptoms of something as dramatic as syphilis.

The emotions, too, offer symptoms of deeper difficulties.

*Some examples:*

excessive daydreaming
nail-biting
skin trouble
poor memory
inability to take any kind of criticism
a low opinion of the opposite sex
obvious negligence about one's clothes

In the catalog of emotional problems, there are literally thousands of symptoms. They may appear to be mental or physical, acute or chronic. A symptom may be obvious or it may go unnoticed by others as well as by onself. But however they appear, and whether or not they are understood for what they are, symptoms constitute warning signs of some inner difficulty.

**What is narcissism?**

Narcissus, according to Greek myth, was a handsome youth. Seeing his reflection for the first time in a pool of water, he became inspired with love for it. Leaning over the pool to look more closely at his image, he fell into the water and was drowned. Today, psychology uses the term "narcissist" to describe any unduly self-centered person.

All children, when quite young, are narcissists. They look for many of their satisfactions within themselves. They are, for instance, in love with their own bodies. They examine themselves constantly, and thoroughly enjoy the various physical functions that life permits them. In this stage, the child sees itself as the center of the world in which it lives. It is all too willing to receive the love of the people in that world. But it is unable to give more than a token of its own love in return.

For many people, this particular phase of self-love is prolonged into adult life. It is a characteristic of men and women whom we usually think of as being egotistical or "stuck on themselves." To such a man, for instance, his own personality and his own actions and qualities are of the highest importance. Narcissism is present to a great degree in those who find themselves unable really to fall in love.

There is some measure of narcissism in all of us. It is the spur that drives us on to look more attractive, to excel at sports or learning, or even to want a better car than our neighbor. It may express itself, perhaps, in the choice of a barber (he gives us exactly the kind of haircut we want); the choice of a college (the best families send their sons there, or it has a first-rate football team); or even in the choice of a mate (all the men in town turn around to look at her).

## What is a defense mechanism?

There are many kinds of defense mechanisms, but all of them have a single aim. They help a person to evade some painful fact about himself, and to present a better "front" to his world. Largely unconscious in origin, a defense mechanism may reveal itself in a man's dreams as well as in his conscious thoughts, feelings and behavior.

It is a sort of compromise. When a powerful unconscious drive in the individual is taboo, and seeks to show itself in spite of that, it collides with another force in the mind. This second force is the individual's sense of responsibility to the demands of society. It recognizes that society (or even the individual himself) would take a harsh view of the unconscious desire in its original form.

As a result, there is a kind of truce between the two forces. The drive is allowed to show itself, but only in some acceptable disguise. The personality of the average human being is capable of many different disguises, and wherever we find a different disguise, we find a different kind of defense mechanism.

*For example:* Does a man hate his father? He knows this is wrong. In his conscious life, therefore, this feeling is translated into some other form. It becomes a hatred for the President of the United States, for the poor (or the rich), for his boss, or even for the New York Yankees. He has thus displaced the original hatred onto something which is considerably more acceptable to himself and others as an object of strong dislike.

*Another example:* Does a man have strong homosexual feelings? Society says that these are "bad." He may then cover up by consciously feeling a strong sense of loathing for homosexuals. Any contact with such people, or even any discussion of them, will disgust him. He has thus reversed the original feeling so that it appears to be its exact opposite.

*One more example:* Does a man fear the responsibilities of being an adult? But society tends to frown on grown-ups who hang onto the privileges of childhood. Such a man may therefore resort to spending much of his adult life as an invalid. Any of a wide variety of ailments may attack him, reducing him to inactivity. As a result of his condition, he will not be expected to assume adult responsibilities—"Can't you see I'm sick?"—and he will receive the kind of attention he most desires. He has, in effect, reverted to the condition of being an infant.

Every normal person is able to use many kinds of defense mechanisms in order to strike a compromise between what he would like to do and what his environment will permit him to do. Repression, Sublimation, Projection, Introjection and Reaction-Formation are some of these protective devices. They are discussed in the following pages.

It should be noted that an individual does not choose a defense mechanism consciously. The selection is dictated entirely by the unconscious mind.

**What is repression?**

Repression is an important means of self-protection in the life of each of us. It keeps us from having to face those innermost feelings and ideas which are too painful or disagreeable for us to bear.

There are people, for example, who may have a deeply buried urge to steal; others may have an urge to be a "peeping Tom," or perhaps to attack someone very close to them. These ideas, however, are so intolerable to the conscious sense of what is right that they are submerged. They are kept in exile in the unconscious portion of the mind.

But these repressed feelings and ideas, though hidden from our conscious awareness, remain active and powerful in the underground of the mind. Here, too, we are not consciously able to control them. They are like black sheep of a good family which lives in a nice, quiet neighborhood. Because of their disreputable character, they have been banished from the home of this family. But the black sheep have smuggled themselves into the basement of the house in spite of this. There, out of sight, they now make themselves at home. And, unknown to the family upstairs, they are able to make a considerable amount of mischief with the furnace, the fuse box, the boiler, and other facilities directly affecting the family's way of life.

Repression is a kind of self-censorship that takes place in the mind of each of us without our own knowledge. By means of it, we are able to hide from ourselves those deep wishes and desires which are socially unacceptable. It helps each of us to keep his own conscious picture of himself from being tarnished.

Freud considered the concept of repression to be one of the fundamental ideas of psychoanalysis.

**What is sublimation?**

Sublimation is the unconscious process by which our deep-seated and powerful drives that are antisocial in nature are detoured into socially acceptable channels.

This is a healthy and constructive process, and everyone makes use of it. It represents one way in which a bargain is arranged between the unruly demands of the unconscious and the lawful standards of the world in which we work and live. Through sublimation, strong unconscious desires which may be immoral or unethical are made to appear in our lives in a more acceptable form. Not only may our environment learn to tolerate the disguised form in which the original desire makes its appearance, but it may even whole-heartedly applaud it.

*For example:* An infant thinks nothing of throwing things around a room and even breaking them. It enjoys the feeling of its own strength. As it grows older, it learns that this urge to destroy must be curbed. By the time the child has arrived at manhood, this energy may have been directed into some path which society views more agreeably. The process of sublimation has begun.

Such a man may be led to seek an army career, where a premium is put on excellence in destruction. He may become a prize fighter or football player, and in either of these cases there may be sizable rewards in the form of money or glory. Or he may become preoccupied with chess, a game in which the urge to hurt or destroy can be intellectualized.

These are some of the ways in which sublimation may transform one kind of antisocial drive. For other antisocial drives it may provide other, equally effective transformations.

### What is projection?

Projection is a technique by which we are able to blame others for our own faults. Each of us uses it to some extent, since practically every one of us finds it necessary, on occasion, to protect his sense of self-esteem. Neurotic persons tend to use this weapon frequently, and to extremes.

Here is how it works: A man may say to his wife, "You don't really love me," and honestly believe the truth of what he is saying. Actually, however, unknown to himself, he may be the one who has ceased to love. He has "projected" onto his wife the fault which he is unable to acknowledge in himself.

The urge to "project" may operate in many types of situations, and always without our realizing that it is at work. But whenever it is used, it always serves the same purpose: It protects us from having to face in ourselves certain qualities, attitudes or feelings about which we are not proud. And it protects us from having to feel guilty about them.

When we are overawed by the boss, it is easier to accuse some other employees of being this way than to have to face the fact of our own feelings. When we are too thrifty to pick up the check when dining out with friends, it is comforting to be able to attribute stinginess to someone else at the table. Or when we are attracted to some woman who is not our wife, it is soothing to be able to accuse another of having those feelings.

Projection permits us to disguise the truth about ourselves by using someone else as a scapegoat. It is no doubt similar to what the Bible implies with the question posed in Luke: "And why beholdest thou the mote that is in thy brother's eye, but perceivest not the beam that is in thine own eye?"

### What is introjection?

Introjection is the process by which a person absorbs feelings, desires, ideas and emotional attitudes from the world around himself. As a child, he may take in from his parents certain views of right and wrong. He takes as his own, usually without question, the belief that the religion of his parents is the only correct one.

As he grows up, a man may take his political ideas from his boss, his ideas from a friend he admires, and his personal prejudices from the group in which he moves. He does not, as a rule, "think" about this process of assimilation.

All through life, each of us continues to accumulate many ideas, desires and points of view from those around us. Everyone's development owes something to this process. When the environment has been a healthy one, the result is good. When the environment has been unhealthy, the individual's personality reflects that, too.

**What is a reaction-formation?**

An unmarried woman with powerful sexual desires may hide such feelings from herself and from the world by playing the role of a prude. Consciously, she may feel disgusted or even outraged by anything even remotely connected with sex.

Or: A man has been rejected and hurt in childhood by the neglect of a mother who had little time for him. He may disguise his underlying resentment by acting like a dutiful and affectionate son. He may even give up the idea of marriage for himself, and devote his entire life to taking care of his mother's needs.

These are examples of reaction-formation, a type of unconscious camouflage. It is a defensive trick for making forbidden desires in ourselves seem (to us and to everyone else) the opposite of what they really are. Our unconscious mind "reacts" to the unpleasantness of the unconscious feeling, and "forms" an image of this feeling in reverse. This helps the individual to exist more serenely in a world of commandments, laws and taboos.

The average man tries as hard as possible to hide his antisocial attitudes from himself and from the people around him. Through a reaction-formation, he is able to act as though the opposite (and more acceptable) attitude or feeling were really true of himself.

Suppose, for example, he has a strong urge to inflict pain on other people. He may then mask this sadistic desire by appearing overly solicitous about the physical comfort of the men and women he meets. He thus finds it easy to believe that his outward, conscious behavior is an honest expression of his real self.

**What is rationalization?**

This is a method by which a person justifies to himself (or to others) certain of his thoughts, feelings and acts with which he might otherwise find fault.

Everyone has some kind of ideal of himself which indicates to him how he ought to be. But an ideal is not always easy to live up to. When a person strays from his ideal, he very often feels an unconscious need to excuse this betrayal of the way he thinks he ought to be. The result is that he invents plausible (but not honest) reasons to excuse himself.

If he suffers a slip of the tongue, which is insulting to a friend or acquaintance, he may call it an accident. If he cheats on his income tax return, he may try to justify this with the claim that "everybody does it." In both cases, he is rationalizing.

Like projection, rationalization is a way of distorting the facts. It acts as a kind of devious lawyer for our defense. It is a technique which makes easier the individual's day-by-day job of living with himself. But the more frequently one needs to rationalize, the more likely it is that one is neurotic.

**What is identification?**

Identification is an unconscious process which helps us to model our attitudes on those of someone we admire. It is a convenient means of pacifying our unfulfilled desires, and it is extremely common.

*For example:* A boy will make use of this process very obviously when he imitates a cowboy star, a ball player, or perhaps his own father.

A girl may be making just as obvious use of it while playing with her doll. She may carefully imitate the way her mother takes care of the baby.

A grown woman will often affect the dress, the hair-do, or even the presumed habits of some movie star. And when the late Clark Gable appeared in one scene of a movie, years ago, minus an undershirt, millions of American men dispensed with wearing their own.

Many people take on, painlessly, the social attitudes and opinions of the person they happen to love. The person with whom one identifies oneself may be anyone at all, from a notorious gangster to a modern saint.

Most people who experience a sense of family feeling, or team spirit, derive from this unity with others a feeling of identification. This is also true of many who belong to organizations like the Elks, the American Legion, or any other kind of closely welded group.

### What is ambivalence?

When we love someone, we like to believe that we love without any qualification. This is certainly the way most people feel about their love for a father or mother, a mate, a child, or any other person really close to them.

But psychoanalysis, which deals largely with the below-the-surface facts about people, says it is only very rarely that we love completely. The contrary, psychoanalysis maintains, is not only entirely possible, but is frequently true. A person may, at one time, have two opposite and conflicting feelings for the same person or thing.

This quirk of the mind is known as ambivalence. It permits the opposing feelings of love and hate to live side by side in the unconscious mind of the same person, both feelings aimed at the same object.

The love we feel for someone may show itself freely enough, and we are usually only too glad to admit it for what it is. But the underlying hatred for this same person may break into the open at times, as well. When this happens, however, the evidence of these darker feelings is likely to be excused away, or simply ignored.

*For example:* A child may show its ambivalence toward its father when it blurts out in one aggrieved moment that it hates him, and in the next that it loves him.

A man may show it by never letting his wife know when he will be detained at the office.

A woman may show it by constantly nagging her husband.

Then there is the fairly common example of the young married couple who seem to be very obviously in love with each other. But, despite this, they spend a good deal of time, just as obviously, fighting with each other.

Life affords people many opportunities for the display of this particular mental process. The newspapers, now and then, offer glaring examples of ambivalence: A mother has strangled her baby because, she says, "It cried too much." Or a man has shot his wife or girl friend after a disagreement over how to spend an evening. To the police, the man insists that "I loved her very much."

In our own lives, most of us occasionally become involved in difficulties with those we think we love or like. The reasons may seem oddly trivial and especially hard to understand. It may be an unfortunate slip of the tongue, for instance. The wrong remark is made, a listener's feelings are hurt, and the speaker cannot understand how he came to say such a thing. "I don't really think that at all," he says to himself. But unknown to himself, part of him actually does feel that way. That is ambivalence.

**What is conversion?**

This is one of the means by which an unconscious desire which has been prevented from expressing itself may show itself nevertheless. It "converts" itself into a physical symptom.

All the emotional energy centered in the original feeling has been dammed up in the unconscious mind. Suddenly, it breaks through this barrier, and shows itself in some less recognizable form. It makes this appearance in the physical life of the individual.

*For example:* A man is forced regularly to endure the company of someone close to him whom he really doesn't like. He then suffers from headaches.

A boy is sent away from home for the first time, to school. Shortly after arriving at the school, he develops a severe illness.

A man in sound physical condition, driven by his urge to get ahead at the office, suddenly comes down with an ulcer.

These examples are simple, and they are few. But there are many other ways in which repressed feelings may convert their energies into physical symptoms.

**What is "the return of the repressed"?**

When we have repressed some taboo feeling or desire, the repressed feeling does not lie quietly in exile, in the unconscious. It strives continually to assert itself—to force itself into our conscious lives—in a variety of ways.

But our inner apparatus for censoring such taboo material is quite strong. It is therefore necessary for the repressed feeling to disguise itself, if it hopes to make an appearance in our consciousness. It does this by exposing itself as a symptom of some kind. The symptom may appear in the form of a dream, a slip of the tongue, a sense of depression, or in one of a thousand other ways.

Some time before, the original taboo feeling was repressed. It was driven beyond the pale of consciousness. Now, wearing some convenient disguise, it has returned to consciousness in the form of a symptom. It was to this process that Freud applied the term "the return of the repressed."

**What is suppression?**

Suppression is a *conscious* method used by everyone to control certain wishes and desires. It is not to be confused with repression, which is an *unconscious* method of control.

*For example:* A man has wanted all his life to be a concert pianist. In the midst of his studies, however, he falls head over heels in love with a girl and marries her. Soon after that, he becomes the father of a family. Because there is not enough money in the house, he is forced to put aside his concert ambitions and get a job in a jazz band. In this way, he has consciously "suppressed" his desire to be a serious pianist. He knows that he has done so in order to support his loved ones.

It is very possible for this same man, of course, to suffer also from repression. He may unconsciously resent the necessity to curb his ambition just because he has to support a wife and children. And his resentment (repressed) may show itself in a dream, or nightmare, in which he destroys his entire family.

**What is a conflict?**

By dictionary definition, a conflict is any contest of opposing forces. This is exactly what psychoanalysts mean when they use the term in describing the emotions.

In the individual, two separate desires or tendencies may exist side by side, at war with each other. They may be conscious or unconscious. But the closer the battle is to being unconscious, the more likely is the struggle to be a bitter one. And the more drastic the results in the personality of the individual.

In civilized society, with its rules, laws, and obligations, conflict lies all around us.

*For example:* A child would like to watch television, but he knows that he must do his homework.

A man may detest his superior at the office, but he may feel forced to invite the man into his home for dinner anyway.

A succession of red traffic lights makes it look as though we will be late to an appointment; the temptation is great to step on the gas and breeze through the lights, but we usually don't.

A man who wishes to go to the ball game on a summer afternoon when he must work in an office, has a conflict of desires. His sense of duty may win out, in which case he remains at his desk. Or, inventing some excuse, he may shirk his duty or obligation to the job and go off to the ball park. In this case, regardless of his decision, the conflict has been a conscious one. He has been aware of it.

This same man may have deeply aggressive instincts. They may be far below the level of his consciousness. He would not believe anyone who suggested that he might have these feelings. These very uncivilized desires demand satisfaction. They lust for "blood." Primitive, childlike, and thoughtless about consequences, they would ordinarily express themselves by physical violence. Without realizing it himself, that man might enjoy the idea of punching his boss, his friend, even his father or his own wife.

Arrayed against these desires, in the same man, are the forces of law and order. These are linked with his sense of decency, of what is "right." The immature urge to satisfy his deeply felt hates clashes with the desire to crush any such violent and antisocial tendency. Here, the conflict takes place in the man's unconscious mind.

In the course of this struggle, the man becomes painfully conscious of the fact that everything is not as it should be with him. He endures a state of tension, without understanding the hidden reasons for it.

When this happens, he is in trouble.

## Dreams

### What did our ancestors think of dreams?

EVER SINCE HIS BEGINNINGS, man has dreamed, and he has always given a special place to his dreams. We find them mentioned in mythology, in the Bible, and in the literature of practically all the peoples of the earth.

Right down to the present century, dreams were almost invariably believed to be prophecies of future events.

The Egyptians of long ago wrote many books on dream interpretation, and experts in this field were highly regarded. In the Old Testament, we know, Joseph won the confidence of Pharaoh by interpreting a dream for him. The prophet Daniel, somewhat later, performed the same service for Nebuchadnezzar, King of Babylon, and won a similar reward.

Among the Greeks, some twenty-five hundred years before Freud, an Athenian citizen named Lysimachus, according to the historian Plutarch, "used to sit near what is called the Iaccheum, and sustained himself by a table for interpreting dreams."

About the same period, also in Greece, Herodotus was noting that "dreams are made up mainly of matters that have been in the dreamer's thoughts during the day." This was a surprisingly practical view of the subject. Two centuries after Herodotus, another Greek, Theocritus, offered another view which was very close to present-day ideas: "In sleep every dog dreams of food, and I, a fisherman, dream of fish." This contains at least a hint of the psychoanalytic view that dreams are based on some wish of the dreamer.

Later still among the Greeks, Artemidorus wrote an entire book on the subject of dreams and their meanings.

Perhaps the most realistic early view of dreams, from the standpoint of modern psychoanalysis, was expressed in the sixteenth century by Montaigne. Here is what the famous French essayist wrote about them: "Dreams are the true interpreters of our inclinations; but there is art required to sort and understand them."

Dreams are a common human experience and, to most people, a mysterious one. For these reasons, large numbers of men and women in every generation have yearned for help in making sense of them. In this country today, and in other countries as well, many books reach print which profess to interpret dreams according to the prophetic rules of the ancients. And many "dream counselors" practice the old art of divining the future from the dreams of the superstitious and insecure. Despite the advances of the twentieth century, far more people have their dreams interpreted in this way than by the methods of psychoanalysis.

**Why are dreams analyzed?**

Among our ancestors (and even among many people of today) dreams were usually thought to offer some magical quality of revelation. (See above.) If their secrets could only be understood, it was believed, they could tell much. Psychoanalysis maintains that our elders were wiser than they knew. An individual's dreams are in fact very revealing, but not in the way our ancestors assumed.

Dreams, according to Freud, are the "royal road to the unconscious." The interpretation of dreams is an essential tool of psychoanalysis, and it permits the unlocking of many secret doors.

Anyone who has ever been around people while they were drinking heavily knows that alcohol loosens the tongue. People tend to say things while drunk that it would never occur to them to say while sober. Often enough, in such a condition, they will reveal only too bluntly exactly what their real feelings are about someone or something.

In his dreams, too, a man finds an opportunity to tell the truth about himself. While he is asleep, his wishes, fears and hopes, buried deep in his unconscious, make their appearance in a kind of playlet. Sometimes this little drama seems to tell a complete story. At other times, it is merely a disjointed series of actions or images. And sometimes it is only some isolated fragment of an image, with no apparent relationship to anything. But always, whatever the dream, it has some kind of significance for the dreamer.

During the day, an element of censorship controls the mind of each of us. Certain of our wishes and fears, because they would never be tolerated by polite society, are kept locked away in the unconscious part of the mind. They are beyond our conscious awareness. But while we are asleep, the vigilance of the censoring element in each of us is relaxed.

The wishes and fears are like criminals which have been kept in prison during the day. At night, while the gatekeeper drowses, they are able to sneak past him. But they can do this only if they are disguised as anything but what they actually are—wishes and fears which the individual does not like to face in himself. They therefore act out their meaning as if they were something quite different, in the form of symbols.

When the analyst and the patient, in cooperation, have uncovered the secret of a particular dream, its real meaning brings the patient a step closer to an understanding of himself.

### What do dreams mean?

"Whenever we sleep," wrote Freud, "we cast off our . . . morality like a garment, only to put it on again in the morning." Every dream has as its central idea the fulfillment of some wish on the part of the dreamer. It is a means of permitting each of us to satisfy, in his sleep, "immoral" or even terrifying wishes and desires of which we are not consciously aware.

The characters and events in a dream are sometimes logical and obvious. But more often they are likely to be mystifying and even incoherent. Even when a dream's meaning appears to be perfectly clear, it usually means something quite different from what it seems to mean. The obvious meaning is usually an ingenious disguise for the real meaning of the dream.

*For example:* A man dreams that he is having a few romantic moments with the woman he loves. Suddenly he becomes aware that the clothes he is wearing are far from modern. He is dressed in a fashion which was popular in the England of a long time ago. Glancing at his reflection in a nearby mirror, he notices that he now resembles Henry the Eighth.

The interpretation of this dream may show the man that it means something far different from an enjoyment, in costume, of a tender moment with the woman he loves. The all-important fact in the dream is that he pictures himself as Henry the Eighth. The dreamer, in this way, sees himself as a man notorious for having killed a number of his wives. Through the dream, he has been able to act out feelings of hatred for the woman he thinks, consciously, that he passionately loves. Other details in the dream may produce equally startling revelations about the nature of the dreamer's real feelings.

A dream is like a remark which carries a double meaning. Its real meaning, or innuendo, lies hidden beneath the surface of what it seems to say. There is a reason for this, and it has already been noted. (See above.) While we are awake, the censoring element in the mind of each of us is also very much awake. It stands guard over our distasteful or painful wishes and thoughts. They are imprisoned deep in our minds, out of the way of consciousness. With the coming of sleep, this censorship is less alert. It remains sufficiently strong, however, to force the hidden wishes, which seek to show themselves, to do so only in a kind of masquerade.

"A dream," Freud wrote, "is the disguised fulfillment of a repressed wish; it is a compromise between the demands of a repressed impulse and the resistance of a censoring force in the ego. . . ."

**Do all dreams have some meaning?**

Yes.

No matter how unimportant a particular dream may appear to be, it has some special meaning. Most dreams stem from some deeply buried cause which is not apparent to the dreamer while he is awake.

But some dreams may seem to have an obvious cause, when remembered on awakening. Dreams which appear to have soothed or exaggerated some simple physical yearning of the night—hunger, thirst, or a too-cold or too-hot temperature in the room, perhaps—are examples. Even such dreams, however, are more significant than they seem to be at first thought. The unconscious, as is its custom, has seized upon the conscious circumstances of the present to act out a little story which may have its real origins in the past.

*For example:* A man dreams that he is stranded in the desert. He is dying of thirst, and the experience is acutely painful to him. Far off on the horizon, there is someone whom he can barely see. He is sure it is a woman and that she will be able to give him water, but he cannot seem to get to her. He awakens, feeling very thirsty.

Since the man was actually quite thirsty before going to bed, it is not surprising that he should dream of being without water in the middle of a desert. His physical condition has stimulated the dream. But his unconscious mind has supplied its own less obvious details. The woman who is beyond reach for him, for instance, may represent his mother, his wife, or even all women in general. What is significant for the dreamer is that he sees a woman who is unreachable, who withholds from him something that he feels he needs and wants.

And of course, when the dream has been completely analyzed, it may be discovered that what he really needs and wants is not really water.

**Why do we dream in symbols?**

We dream in symbols for just about the same reason that children are often taught to speak in symbols.

Many parents encourage their children to use baby-talk synonyms to describe natural functions or parts of the body. There are certain kinds of actions and things—elimination and sex organs are examples—about which these parents have a feeling of distaste, at least as far as conversation is concerned.

Children are notoriously free with language, and such a parent, perhaps dreading eventual embarrassment, will therefore educate his child to use synonyms or code words for what the child really means. The child is thus taught to speak about certain things in a very private language.

Our dreams use symbols for a similar reason. The pressure of the unconscious to "tell all" while we are asleep, is countered by sleepy but still existent pressure from the conscious to "tell nothing." (See above.) The result is a secret language (like the child's code words) which we know as symbols.

Not all dreams, as most people are aware, are in the form of stories or incidents. Sometimes we may dream about a single image or even object, rather than about something that "happens." The content of the dream may simply be a view of an office building, a man sitting on a suitcase, an old pair of shoes, or a hospital thermometer.

In this kind of dream we have simply "condensed" a great many ideas into one. This single image is like a very brief and colorless telegram which is meant to describe a complicated and even extremely interesting event. And the bare bones of the telegram, in a manner of speaking, require expert translation. It is the function of analysis to decipher the meaning of this condensed version of what the unconscious is trying to say.

When we dream, the unconscious is able to dress itself in a large variety of other disguises, in order to obscure its real meaning. It can telescope time, so that incidents which are years apart in one's experience seem to be taking place at the same moment. In a particular dream it may "displace" the emphasis of persons and events. The things which are important to us may appear to be quite trivial. And the reverse of this is just as likely to happen.

Our unconscious is able even to use puns to hide its real meaning from us. And it can use them in every language with which we are familiar.

In a way, a dream is like a piece of bone found in some remote area. The layman who discovers it may guess that it comes from some animal, probably a large animal. But the expert in prehistoric zoölogy may recognize the bone immediately as part of the left hind foot of a certain type of dinosaur. From this single clue, he may be able to reconstruct the entire animal.

A psychoanalyst, with the help of the patient, is usually able to do as much with a dream.

### Is every dream based on a wish?

According to Freud, the answer is a positive Yes. "In every dream," he wrote, "an instinctual wish is displayed as fulfilled." He allowed for no exceptions.

The dreams of children, he pointed out, are usually very simple and uncomplicated examples of how some wishes achieve easy gratification through the medium of the dream. The dreams of adults, of course, are far more complex. In them, the wish of the dreamer may not be very apparent.

Some people will be reminded, here, that they have had dreams (or even nightmares) in which they were being literally beaten, punished, frightened, or otherwise made extremely unhappy. Their legitimate question would be: Where is the wish in such a dream?

Even in this kind of a dream, according to Freud, there is, in its own way, the secret expression of a wish. It is not one of the instincts for pleasure which is being gratified here, but one's conscience. What is in evidence is the working of that portion of the mind which seeks to censure or criticize the dreamer for having some wish that is taboo. When this kind of dream is analyzed, it becomes possible to discover what the buried wish was. It is then made clear why the dream of punishment or anxiety was inflicted on the dreamer.

A French proverb tells us that there is no pillow so soft as a clear conscience. This is one version of the widely recognized assumption that when a person feels guilty, he is unlikely to sleep well. An unpleasant dream is one way in which a guilty conscience can make us pay for an antisocial wish.

**Do daydreams mean anything?**

Yes.

When a normal person has a daydream, it can at times lead to some kind of action. The daydream, in this way, can act as a source of invention for a scientist, it can inspire a poet or artist, give a new sales idea to a businessman, or provide a cooking idea for a housewife. It can even, for some of us, suggest a good joke suitable for passing along to our friends. The normal person never loses his sense of reality in the course of the daydream.

The neurotic person, on the other hand, very easily becomes lost in his fantasy. It becomes for him a substitute for doing something, rather than a path to action or even a merely occasional form of idling. In his daydream, the neurotic usually plays an enjoyable role. This is, for him, a satisfactory end in itself. His daydream represents things as he would like them to be. It becomes for him a substitute for reality, which represents things as they actually are.

James Thurber's famous short story, "The Secret Life of Walter Mitty," offers a good example of this kind of daydream. In his mind, Mitty is constantly engaged in attempts to escape the reality of his humdrum and even oppressive existence. He has daydreams in which he imagines himself in turn a heroic naval commander, a famous surgeon, and a tight-lipped, intrepid infantry officer.

There is a direct connection between the emotional problems of a neurotic person and the particular kind of daydreams he is likely to have.

**Can dreams be interpreted by a nonprofessional?**

Since man first began to dream, there have been men willing to analyze his dreams for him. These men have not always been qualified to do so. Even today, it is not difficult to find a friend who will volunteer to explain the meaning of one's dream. Despite the fact that such interpretations often seem quite plausible, they are unlikely to be more than superficially correct.

An informed layman is often able to understand the meaning of the limited number of dream symbols which usually—*but not always*—represent the same things. But there remain an unlimited number of other symbols. These are so personal to the dreamer that their meaning has to be groped for. They can be revealed only after following the dreamer's free associations to the particular symbol.

This is a job which requires the skill of a trained professional.

The more obvious meaning of a dream can sometimes be surmised correctly by a man or woman well-read in psychoanalysis. But the underlying meaning is almost certain to escape such an interpreter. And it is this underlying meaning which has special significance for the dreamer.

When a nonprofessional interprets someone's dream, even on the most friendly and helpful basis, it may have harmful results. By putting emphasis where it does not belong, he may encourage the dreamer to preoccupy himself with ideas which have no real bearing on his problem.

Freud himself is supposed to have remarked on one occasion that "sometimes a cigar is only a cigar." This was one way of warning against too hasty or even uninformed interpretations.

## The Men Who Treat the Patient

### How many psychoanalysts are there in the United States?

THE LARGEST BODY of medically trained psychanalysts in this country is the American Psychoanalytic Association, which has approximately a thousand members. The analysts who belong to this association are devoted to the principles expounded by Sigmund Freud. There are perhaps an equal number of psychoanalysts (also with medical backgrounds) who are not associated with this group. (See page 134.)

In comparison:

There are about twelve thousand psychiatrists affiliated with the American Psychiatric Association.

The American Psychological Association lists eighteen thousand member psychologists. It has been estimated that there are perhaps six thousand other psychologists in this country who are not affiliated with this association.

According to the American Medical Association, there are well over 200,000 M.D.'s presently involved in some phase of physical medicine in the United States.

### Have all analysts themselves been analyzed?

Yes.

There are two important reasons for this.

First, the very nature of analysis makes it necessary to assure the patient a sense of privacy during treatment. Thus, unlike other forms of medical study, it is virtually impossible to demonstrate an actual psychoanalysis before a group of students. As a result, the student can really learn the technique only by undergoing analysis himself.

Second, every analyst must be able to approach the

problems of the patient with complete objectivity. He must be able to remain emotionally detached from the difficulties which beset the patient he is treating. The only way he can insure this is by ridding himself of his own tendencies to neurotic thinking and behavior. And the only way for him to accomplish *this* is through his own psychoanalysis.

It is for these reasons that a psychoanalyst must be analyzed himself before he can begin practice.

**Are all analysts equally competent?**

No.

Psychoanalysts are no more likely to be equally competent in the treatment of patients than are the members of any other group of medical specialists.

One analyst may enjoy particular success with male patients, whereas another may have greater success with female patients. Some analysts are exceptionally good at handling special kinds of problems: those of creative persons, of alcoholics, or of patients with great feelings of inferiority, for example. Other analysts may be particularly expert in treating other kinds of problems.

Among accredited analysts, any difference in ability, where it exists, is likely to be apparent in terms of specialty, rather than in general qualifications.

**What is the difference between a psychiatrist and a psychoanalyst?**

Psychiatry is that area of medicine which concerns itself with the diagnosis and treatment of mental disorders.

Psychoanalysis, which emphasizes a highly specialized approach to the treatment of mental and emotional problems, is one branch of psychiatry.

A *psychiatrist* is a doctor who, in addition to his general medical education, has had at least three years of instruction and training in psychiatry. Before being licensed to practice, he must have had at least two years of actual experience in psychiatric practice, usually at an institution.

A *psychoanalyst* is a physician who has absorbed the training necessary to qualify as a psychiatrist. But he has spent from four to six additional years in mastering the specific techniques necessary to practice psychoanalysis. During the course of this added learning period, he must have been analyzed himself.

In many people's minds, the two terms—psychiatrist and psychoanalyst—are confused. It is often assumed that they are interchangeable, two ways of saying the identical thing. But:

While every psychoanalyst is also a psychiatrist, the reverse is far less likely to be true. Not many psychiatrists are experienced in psychoanalysis, nor have very many of them been analyzed themselves. A sizable number of them, however, have been influenced to some extent by Freudian methods and ideas.

**What is a lay analyst?**

A lay analyst is a specialist in the treatment of emotional problems who has been trained in the methods of psychoanalysis. But he lacks a medical background, and the prefix "lay" is therefore commonly used to distinguish him from the psychoanalyst who is also an M.D.

Besides postgraduate study and clinical work, a qualified lay analyst has been analyzed himself as a preparation for the practice of psychoanalysis.

There is much controversy among psychoanalysts as to the value of lay analysis. Most of them take the view that their profession is a branch of medicine. Persons without a medical background, they feel, are not qualified to treat problems which are so often intertwined with physical symptoms. (See page 105.)

As additional support for their position, they point to the fact that in most states there are no laws to prevent literally anyone from setting up in practice as a lay analyst. While builders, barbers and even motorists must be duly licensed in most states, those who profess to practice psychoanalysis almost invariably are not. This leaves the door open, many analysts feel, to the abuse of the profession by persons of the most dubious qualifications.

Another point that disturbs many psychoanalysts: there are far too few medically trained analysts to handle the large number of prospective patients who seek help. It is not unusual, for instance, for an analyst (with an M.D.) to have a list of prospective patients who must wait many months, perhaps years, before he can take them under treatment. For this reason, as well as others, many people who feel the need for therapy will seek the services of the lay analyst.

Despite the objections of many of today's psychoanalysts to the practice of lay analysis, Sigmund Freud himself believed that it had value. He said, ". . . it does not matter whether the analyst is a doctor or not, so long as the danger of a mistake . . . is secured against by the prescribed medical opinion before the analysis begins, and, if required, during its course. For [the patient] it is incomparably more important that the analyst should possess such personal qualities as will command his confidence, and that he should have acquired the knowledge and insight, and the experience, which alone can fit him for his task."

Most psychoanalysts will agree, despite their general objections, that some lay analysts have made valuable contributions to the theory and practice of psychoanalysis.

### What is a psychologist?

A psychologist is a specialist in the study of human behavior.

He is concerned with the reasons why people think and act as they do. He may have a doctor's degree in psychology from a school of recognized standing, or he will at least have done graduate work, plus work in the field. Unlike the psychiatrist and the psychoanalyst, he does not have a medical degree.

Depending on his particular training, a psychologist may be able to offer any of the following services: educational and vocational guidance; marital counseling; testing of individual intelligence, as well as personality. Psychologists are widely used in personnel and educational work. They also perform many clinical and research functions.

A "clinical psychologist" may practice psychotherapy (see page 81) but few clinical psychologists treat their patients according to the theories of Freudian psychoanalysis.

**Do psychoanalysts take charity cases?**

Yes.

Like other members of the medical profession, many psychoanalysts take care of patients who need treatment but cannot afford it. Such treatment is often made available through institutes which have been set up for the training of psychoanalysts.

**Are there quacks who call themselves psychoanalysts?**

Yes.

Fakers can manage to find their way into any profession ministering to people who need help. As in law, medicine, religion, and other fields, psychoanalysis also has its quota of unauthorized practitioners.

This kind of fraud is made especially easy by the lack of effective legislation to control the practice of psychoanalysis. In very few parts of the country is there any real attempt to restrict the field to duly qualified persons. In some states it is legally possible for a person to set up practice as a "psychoanalyst" without even a grade school education.

Trade names such as "psychological counselor" or

"psychologist" are also freely adopted in many areas. The people who take on these titles are often qualified to do so only by the weakness of local laws.

The problem of the faker who offers false guidance for profit is hardly a new one. Dante wrote his *Inferno* almost seven hundred years ago, and in the course of the writing, he may have had just such quacks in mind. In his vision of hell, the poet described nine separate circles in which different types of sinners are tormented with increasingly sadistic punishments. In the eighth circle, being consumed and reconsumed by flames, he placed "'evil counselors."

**How can one tell that a psychoanalyst is not a quack?**

A qualified psychoanalyst is usually a member of an accredited psychoanalytical society. Such groups are to be found in every part of the United States. At the very least, any real doctor's background and education can be checked in an official medical register.

The best way to find out if an analyst is qualified is to write a letter of inquiry to the secretary of the psychiatric or psychoanalytic society closest to home. The address may usually be secured from the offices of any county medical society or local hospital.

## The Patient and the Analysis

### What is psychotherapy?

PEOPLE HAVE HAD nervous or emotional problems since soon after they began to inhabit this world. Any means devised by man to cope with such problems is, generally speaking, a form of psychotherapy. The term is an all-embracing one. Even an African witch doctor practices a form of psychotherapy when he tries to remove the spell which may be bothering one of his clients.

Such different approaches as faith healing, the advice and reassurance of a respected friend, and professional psychiatric attention, are only a few of the many forms of treatment which might be called psychotherapy.

Modern medicine, however, has narrowed the meaning of the word. Specifically, it now includes only those forms of treatment requiring the attention of someone qualified by training to handle nervous and emotional problems. Clinical psychologists and psychiatrists, for instance, practice forms of psychotherapy.

Psychoanalysis is only one of the specialized techniques in this field.

### How does psychoanalysis differ from other kinds of psychotherapy?

Compared with other forms of psychotherapy, psychoanalysis tends to probe more deeply into the mind and life of the individual.

It deals primarily with the causes of the patient's problems, and these causes are the central target of treatment. Other types of psychotherapy, however, focus largely on the patient's symptoms. By learning to understand these symptoms, it is felt, the patient is encouraged to face his problems more intelligently.

In analysis, the patient learns not only to face his problems, but how best to deal with them. Also, with the help of his doctor, the patient does most of the work. In other forms of psychotherapy, in contrast, the therapist usually plays a far more active part. As a rule, he is not especially interested in exploring too deeply the background of the patient's problems. And, unlike the analyst, he provides the patient with a great deal of suggestion and advice to help him cope with the problems he faces "now." The therapist may also spend a considerable amount of time simply talking with the patient, trying to prop up his sense of self-esteem.

It has been said of the psychoanalyst that he "dives deeper, stays down longer, and comes up dirtier" than any other therapist. Analysts point to these features as being exactly the ones which provide the special benefits of psychoanalytic treatment. It is the only type of psychotherapy, they claim, which can be expected to produce a real change in the patient.

**What is the best age at which to be psychoanalyzed?**

The man or woman who can profit from analysis should enter treatment as soon as possible. Psychoanalysts support this view by an elementary point of logic: The years after a successful analysis may provide the individual with a satisfying and constructive life; the years which precede analysis remain unsalvageable for the patient—they have already been lived.

The sooner analysis is begun, therefore, the greater the number of years ahead in which the individual may hope to live his life at the peak of his powers.

**Is age an important factor in analysis?**

Yes.

A successful analysis hinges on two important elements in the patient: He must have some capacity for reasonableness, and his personality must be flexible. While the passing of the years tends to make a person more reasonable, it may also stiffen his inner resistance to change. The younger a person is, the less likely is he to be reasonable but the more likely to be susceptible to change.

The years in which psychoanalysis can hope to accomplish most for the individual are, very roughly, those when he is between twelve and forty-five years of age. But even these limits are by no means arbitrary. While it is difficult to achieve great success with the very young and the very old, remarkable results have been gained with children under twelve. This is also true for people older than forty-five (or even fifty). These latter, of course, lack some of the emotional flexibility of their earlier years. This makes analysis more difficult for them than it might once have been. But even so, some success can still be hoped for.

### How does the patient choose his analyst?

A prospective patient usually chooses his analyst in the same way he might select a dentist, a lawyer, or a family doctor. Perhaps he has read about the analyst somewhere and been impressed by his accomplishments. Or, more likely, a friend of the patient may have told him about the man, recommending him highly.

Again, the analyst may have been chosen from a list of several who have been suggested as possibilities. This list may have been provided by some person or organization to whom the prospective patient has appealed for guidance. Local analytic, psychiatric, or medical societies are usually able to provide the names of specialists in a given community.

During his first, exploratory interview, the patient is encouraged to discuss fees, hours, and even the credentials of the analyst. Complete candor is not only good sense, but it helps to get the analysis off on the right foot. And it is welcomed by the analyst.

The patient's feelings about the analyst at this first

meeting are very important. There is no doubt that a very long string of degrees and clinical associations can do much to reassure the patient. But perhaps even more important is the way he feels about the analyst in the course of that first interview. Progress in treatment is usually more rapid when the patient likes the analyst as a person. If he is able to experience such a sense of warmth at this first meeting, the analysis is likely to be off to a good start. Psychoanalysts agree that this closeness of feeling between patient and analyst is of fundamental importance in the course of treatment.

Note: Unlike a dentist, lawyer, or physician, a psychoanalyst should never be selected from among one's friends. If he is not a complete stranger to the patient, the analyst may lack the objectivity essential to the best treatment. And for the same reason, the patient may indulge in forms of resistance (see page 91) that might not otherwise occur.

**Should a patient select an analyst of his own sex?**

Not necessarily.

Like much else in life, such preferences may be matters of individual taste. Some patients feel more at ease with an analyst of their own sex, while others may prefer an analyst of the opposite sex.

With some patients, the particular emotional problem may determine the choice. The choice, however, is not always made consciously. If it is, the patient will be aware of his preference before treatment has begun. If not, his preference will become known to him soon enough in the course of treatment. He may then change to another analyst, should the wisdom of such a move become apparent.

**What is the basic procedure of psychoanalysis?**

The primary aim of psychoanalysis is to help the patient solve the problems which brought him to treatment. The road to such a solution leads back into the past. In most cases, the roots of these problems lie in the shocks, hurts and grievances of the patient's childhood experiences.

Normally, the patient is not consciously aware of the real origins of his problems. He is inclined to blame them on situations of the moment.

In the course of analysis, the sources of these problems, embedded in his unconscious mind like a kind of emotional infection, are brought into the open. This is done largely through the use of the patient's memory. Through analysis of his dreams, his memory and understanding of himself are stimulated. Much of the time he talks about what has happened to him in the past, and what is happening to him in the present. And through analysis, the patient learns about the evasions and defenses he has built up to keep from having to face his problems.

Slowly, as the patient reconstructs the events of his life, he brings to light the factors and the events which have resulted in his problems of today. He may learn, for instance, that his current attitude toward his job can be traced directly to his childhood attitude toward his father. His feelings about his wife may be linked with his earliest feelings about his mother or sister or both. Even the fact that he seems to prefer poker to dancing may be less a simple matter of taste than he once believed.

By means of psychoanalysis, the patient is able to re-live, at times emotionally, the situations which touched off his deepest problems. It is this re-enactment of his problems, under the guidance of the analyst, that helps the patient to real self-understanding. And it is this real self-understanding, achieved through psychoanalysis, which makes for a "cure."

### What is an analytic session like?

An average psychoanalytic session proceeds somewhat along these lines:

The patient appears at the analyst's office at his appointed time. With a minimum of social preliminaries, he lies down on a couch. The analyst is seated on a chair behind and out of sight of the patient.

The patient then begins to talk of whatever comes into his mind. It may be a dream he has had the night before, a memory or feeling of the moment, even an idle thought. Or it may be some current situation in his daily life which happens to be troubling him. Everything and anything is suitable for discussion. The range of subject matter which may be covered by this talk is considerably wider than the average person is able to realize. And the depth to which it may reach would be equally difficult for him to comprehend.

At some points, the analyst may offer his own interpretations of what is under discussion. At other times he may ask questions. He may even permit the entire period to go by without saying a word.

There may come moments when the patient is silent, seemingly having talked himself out. Neither he nor the analyst is likely to be disturbed by such silences. They have happened before, and they will no doubt happen again. The patient knows he is really "talked out" only when his problems are finally solved.

At the end of his allotted period, the patient leaves. Before he returns for his next appointment, he will spend time thinking of what he has learned about himself. Ideally, he will try to make the most of his new awarenesses about himself. The patient is expected to work on his problems while away from the analyst, as well as with him.

### Why does a patient lie on a couch?

The patient's maximum coöperation, conscious and unconscious, is highly desirable during an analytic session. Lying on a couch is, for many patients, a step in this direction. Any physical tension tends to be relieved, since lying down provides the patient with a sense of conscious relaxation.

Also, unable to see the face of the analyst, he is unlikely to respond to any changes of expression he might otherwise see there. The patient will therefore be more certain to concentrate on his own more pertinent problems.

The analyst, meanwhile, seated to the rear and able to look down on the patient, is in an excellent position to observe every detail of his facial expressions. The interplay of emotions displayed there gives the analyst an additional barometer of the patient's changing feelings in the course of the session.

It should be noted, however, that not all patients use a couch. Some of them, for special reasons, may discuss their problems with the psychoanalyst from an ordinary chair.

**How long does a single analytic session last?**

As a rule, an individual psychoanalytic "hour" lasts fifty minutes. This is true for the vast majority of patients. In exceptional cases, usually depending on the needs or circumstances of a particular patient, the session may be somewhat shorter or even longer.

**How many sessions are required per week?**

The number may vary from a single session per week to as many as six in that same period. This may depend on one or more of a number of factors: The emotional needs of the patient; his ability to pay for extra sessions if indicated; the views of the analyst; and the time schedule of the analyst, the patient, or both.

The more often a patient sees the analyst, the more constant is the pressure put upon his unconscious to give way to the demands of treatment. The less frequent the sessions, the slower the progress made in battering through the wall of unconscious resistance. It is for this reason that some analysts feel that too few sessions per week cannot really justify the term "psychoanalysis." In their view, the pressures of treatment must be constant and unremitting. Otherwise, the forces of resistance within every patient find it only too easy to keep the analysis on an almost superficial level of therapy.

All things considered, the analyst is usually able to judge how often a particular patient should be seen in order to insure his maximum progress.

The average patient's schedule calls for three to five sessions per week.

### Can an analyst predict the length of treatment?

In a very general way, yes.

By the end of the first weeks (or certainly months) of treatment, the analyst's professional insight gives him a fairly clear picture of the problems facing the patient. On this basis he can usually make a good guess as to whether the patient faces a longer or a shorter period in treatment.

The analyst is not likely to inform the patient of this guess, however. To do so might cause the patient to relax his own efforts and look to the analyst to meet a deadline. The analyst would then be expected to produce a "cure" within a time limit which can really be determined only by the patient himself.

### How long does individual analysis take?

There is no set period of time for the completion of an analysis. A conventional form of education—college, for instance—usually requires the same number of years for almost everyone. But psychoanalysis is a far more complicated form of education. The amount of time it requires depends primarily on the individual patient.

Each person has his own problems, and each person has, in addition, a highly individual ability (or inability) to manage those problems. Some patients have been known to derive maximum benefit in a matter of months. Many, however, must continue in treatment for a far longer period of time. If there is such a thing as an "average" period for an analysis, it would be, perhaps, in the neighborhood of 450 hours or sessions.

## Why does analysis take so long?

In terms of the actual number of hours necessary, many people are able to complete a successful analysis in less time than it takes to master a foreign language. A student thinks little of spending several hours a week, for two or three years, in learning how to find his way through French or German fluently. In the same amount of time, or less, a person in analysis is usually able to develop a fluent understanding of himself. And not only is this a far more difficult course of study than any foreign language, but it is considerably more useful as well.

To undergo analysis, the professionals in the field point out, is to undergo a process of education, or more accurately, re-education. Each of us has made for himself a way of life which works, after a fashion. But this individual pattern each of us has developed through the years has been achieved only at the expense of deep personal dissatisfactions.

Much of this dissatisfaction is known to us only in the form of fears, hates, envy, a sense of failure, or any of a great number of other disturbing reactions.

*For example:* That job we have is dull and frustrating, and every day at the office is like another year of ordeal. But there seems to be little we are able to do about the situation.

Perhaps there is the feeling that we married the wrong person. This may result in feelings of guilt, self-pity, anxiety and other weights on the spirit. And through it all, the mind is assailed by recurring barrages of good and bad intentions.

Perhaps the load of responsibilities we carry is too heavy and ungiving a burden. As far as we can see, there appears to be no way to lighten this load. One result of this may be constant feelings of depression.

In each of these situations, our unconscious mind is speaking to us, and it is making its protest. But it speaks a language foreign to us, and having to live within the sound of that language without understanding it, makes for trouble in our lives.

Psychoanalysis seeks to expose the real reasons for the patient's pattern of living—why he thinks, feels and acts as he does. To do this, his unconscious mind must be systematically explored and its secrets made plain. Bit by bit, the patient comes to understand the *why* of his feelings and behavior. And step by step, the inner mechanism which has maintained the balance of power in his life throughout his previous years—his unconscious—fights back at this attempt to get at its secrets. It seeks desperately to hang onto the past, and it fights against the idea of change. It is for this reason that there are no easy victories in psychoanalysis. Every step forward is achieved only as the result of effort and struggle.

Resistance (see below) is the special weapon used by the unconscious in its war against progress in treatment. It is the principal reason why analysis often takes such a long period of time. The simple word "resistance" covers a whole armory of mines, booby traps and road blocks in the human personality. All are aimed at obstructing successful treatment.

During analysis, the mind of the patient is like a vast and complicated battleground on which warfare never ceases. Even in the average patient, the forces of resistance are both tenacious and crafty. They fight hard to hold on to their own.

In view of what must be contended with, many psychoanalysts maintain, it is surprising that treatment does not take an even longer time than it usually does.

**How does resistance work?**

In the words of Freud, resistance is "anything that interferes with the course of analysis." It is the work of the unconscious, which continually sets up barriers in the path of treatment.

Faced with the probings of analysis, the unconscious marshals all its forces to resist a cure. The variety and strength of these forces is considerable.

*For example:* The patient may arrive late for his appointment with the analyst. He may even manage to forget it entirely. In either case, of course, he will be able to provide some "plausible" excuse for his behavior.

He may suddenly find himself unable to remember any of his dreams. This may help him to develop a what's-the-use? feeling about his analysis. Alternatively, he may barrage the analyst with a large number of dreams. These may turn out to be neither especially new nor meaningful in content, but they must be interpreted in a relatively profitless, time-wasting procedure.

The patient may decide to reject certain ideas about himself which he has discovered through analysis. This may permit him to waste an excessive amount of time in thrashing out the merits of his own position during his sessions. He may even find it "profitable" to turn the tables on the analyst, and proceed to analyze *him.*

The patient may find himself going through long periods of silence, his mind a blank. Try as he may, there seems to be absolutely nothing he can think of to say. This sort of thing can make it only too easy for him to convince himself that he might as well stop treatment.

And as a last resort, for any of the above reasons or for others which can easily present themselves to him, the patient can decide that his analysis is just not worth the trouble. He quits.

These are only some of the ways in which resistance may operate. It shows itself constantly in the course of analysis, and it is not always immediately recognized for what it is. But on recognition, it is analyzed. Constant examination of these unconscious attempts to fight off treatment will result, eventually, in the decline of the powers of resistance.

When the fight against the patient's resistance has been won, it is a sign that the analysis is approaching its end.

Note: To get some idea of the capacity of the mind to present obstacles to any attempt to explore it, it might help to understand the staggering complexity of the average human brain. Here is how Dr. J. C. Herrick, a neurologist, has described it: "The human brain is the most complicated structural apparatus known to science. If *all* the equipment of the telegraph, telephone and radio of the North American continent could be squeezed into a half-gallon cup, it would be *less* intricate than the three pints of brains that fill your skull and mine." [Italics supplied.]

**Why is psychoanalysis so expensive?**

Psychoanalysis is expensive for the same reason that a college education is expensive—it takes a great deal of time. And it is expensive, too, for the same reason that surgery is expensive—because the practitioner is required to have a highly specialized background of study and experience.

To undergo psychoanalysis is not as conventional an act as to go to college. If it were, there would probably be much less talk of its expense. It might be noted, incidentally, that the total cost of a college education is often greater than that of a complete analysis. And, unlike college, psychoanalysts claim, the benefits it affords will affect most of the areas of the individual's way of life. And, even more than college, these benefits are likely to last him throughout the remainder of his lifetime.

If psychoanalysis were as obviously dramatic as surgery, few people would be likely to question its cost. A year of analysis may be no more expensive than certain kinds of operations. The results, in terms of the effect on the patient's future life, can often be at least as beneficial—and as noticeable.

The average analytic fee may be anywhere from fifteen to twenty-five dollars per session. There are some cases in which the fee is higher. And there are others, of course, in which it may be lower. Like other doctors, an analyst will at times adjust his fees downward, for the benefit of a needy patient.

Because each session usually lasts for about fifty minutes, the number of patients the analyst can treat in a given period of time is directly limited. Naturally enough, this factor also limits his income. The psychoanalyst is the only medical specialist who is paid, in effect, "by the hour."

A doctor of general medicine is sometimes able to see three or four patients in the time an analyst must spend with only one. And although the individual fees this doctor charges his patients may be less, their total can, often enough, be greater than the fee charged by the analyst in the same period of time. In terms of yearly income, in fact, the psychoanalyst is not too far from the bottom among medical specialists.

Before he is fully prepared to practice, a psychoanalyst can look back on a study period of some fifteen years. Among other medical men, only the surgeon requires that much training. The yearly income of the average surgeon is greater than that of the average psychoanalyst. Also, surgery is often quite expensive, and this fact is accepted without question by the general public. The reason for this acceptance is not hard to find. Surgery has been a readily understandable medical specialty for hundreds of years. Its benefits (and even its expense) are common knowledge to most of us.

Psychoanalysis, in contrast, is comparatively new. Most of the public knows nothing about it. Worse, many people suffer from a considerable misunderstanding of what it is or tries to do. In many minds it seems to breed suspicion or even downright fear. With some people, therefore, any stick will do to cudgel the idea of psychoanalysis, and objection to its cost is certainly one of the more convenient ones.

On the basis of the professional training expected of a qualified analyst—

Plus the amount of attention he is required to give the patient—

Plus the results which may be expected in the average case—

The cost of psychoanalysis compares favorably with that of other branches of medicine.

In recent years, as most people have had occasion to note, all medical costs have been high. Psychoanalysis is no exception.

### Do some patients enter analysis through a desire to be led?

Yes.

Of some patients this is undoubtedly true. They are men and women who, as a rule, lack the courage to make their own decisions. They would like someone else, someone stronger than themselves, to solve their problems for them.

This kind of patient tends to see the analyst as a benign authority, full of understanding and not unlike an ideal parent. Such a patient expects to be led effortlessly along the path he should travel.

The analyst, however, does not lead the patient in this sense. He helps the patient to understand what is right for himself. By the time the patient gets to this point of understanding, he is expected to develop sufficient inner strength to make his way through life under his own power.

**Does the analyst make decisions for the patient?**

Inability to decide on a course of action, and take it, is often a symptom of emotional distress. Psychoanalysis, to be successful, must encourage the patient to stand on his own feet. He must learn not only to make his own decisions but, once having made them, to accept their consequences.

Most people would agree that one of the worst types of failure in life is the man who has never tried to do anything. The fear of failure produces, in many people, a do-nothing attitude toward situations that ordinarily call for some kind of action. Very often this can be worse than failure itself. At the very least, it may smother any expression of initiative or even talent.

In analysis, a patient learns to accept the fact that he may fail in a given line of action. Once he has accepted this possibility, it loses much of its terror for him. As a result, the act of making a decision becomes, for him, less weighted with emotional tension. In time the patient develops a sense of his own strength, a sense of confidence in what he is really able to do for himself.

A mature person is able to make his own decisions. In analysis, the patient who is incapable of this learns by doing. Only in extreme circumstances will an analyst directly make up the patient's mind about something. When this happens, it is, as a rule, only to forestall an unwise decision contemplated by the patient.

*For example:* The patient may decide to leave his job. But this decision is made at the wrong time and for the wrong reasons.

He may suddenly decide that he wants to get married. But he may not be quite ready for so serious a step.

He may convince himself that it is not only wise but also necessary that he should leave his wife and family. But this, should he do it, may have disastrous results.

Any decisive actions, taken without mature consideration, may prove harmful. When the patient seeks to embark, for the wrong reasons, on some action which is headed for trouble, the analyst is likely to try to dissuade him.

On the rare occasions when it becomes necessary, the analyst may offer his own advice.

**Are there more women than men in analysis?**

No.

Despite popular opinion to the contrary, the most recent available survey shows that there are slightly more men than women undergoing psychoanalysis.

**Is hypnosis ever used in analysis?**

Psychoanalysis makes use of hypnosis, but only rarely. It is used by only a minority of analysts, and even these do not use it with every patient.

In a special case, a patient may be put into a trance, either by suggestion or by drugs. This is usually done at some point in the analysis when the patient's ability to respond to treatment seems to be seriously blocked. His unconscious resistance to treatment is effectively barring progress.

Under hypnosis, this especially immovable obstacle may be broken through. The patient is then able to bring into the open the reasons for a significant symptom or feeling. In such circumstances, hypnosis acts as a short cut to the discovery of information. It may thereby save time for the patient and the analyst.

While he is under hypnosis, however, the patient is in an extremely dependent state. His will to action lies inert. In a condition of half-sleep, treatment proceeds with no real effort on his part. The analyst, in effect, does all the work. For this reason, hypnosis is used sparingly, if at all, in psychoanalysis.

Any analysis, in order to be successful, must give the patient a sense of independence. The frequent use of hypnosis would make this goal more difficult to achieve. It would encourage the patient to expect too much of the analyst and too little of himself.

### What is insight?

As any psychoanalysis proceeds, the patient learns more and more about the remote and infantile sources of his attitudes and his behavior. He may learn, for example, just why it is that he is inclined to be self-centered, or tight with money, or filled with feelings of personal inadequacy, or sadistic with women. From time to time he may discover the background reasons for other ways in which he is less "right" than he could be. Each such discovery is a new "insight" into himself.

In the course of analysis, anything which contributes to the patient's self-understanding is called an insight. The path to any degree of improvement in therapy is filled with them.

### Do husband and wife ever have the same analyst?

As a rule, no.

It is not unusual for a husband and wife to be undergoing psychoanalysis during the same period of their lives. But it is relatively uncommon for both of them to undertake it with the same analyst.

Most analysts would object to the idea of treating both husband and wife. It would introduce, they feel, many problems which would not exist if each of the patients were to see separate analysts. The argument against it runs something like this:

All people have problems, and when two people are married, they have special problems with each other. In the course of any psychoanalysis, a great strain is put on the emotional life of the patient. He is almost sure to become very jealous of his personal relations with the analyst. Should he be constantly aware that his wife was also seeing "his" analyst, it would be likely to provoke problems and resistances that might not otherwise occur.

The wife, on her part, would probably be experiencing her own additional difficulties. And in neither case would these problems be likely to intrude, if the couple were seeing separate analysts.

Even under the best of circumstances, the course of therapy is far from smooth. When husband and wife are seeing the same analyst, it is even rougher.

**Is it necessary to tell one's analyst everything?**

Yes.

All of the patient's thoughts, feelings, dreams and even casual comments, are usable material in the process of psychoanalysis. In many instances, the patient may be the poorest possible judge of what is worth discussing in his treatment.

The patient is expected, in every one of his sessions, to tell all that comes consciously to mind. Only in this way can he hope to make headway against the formidable censorship imposed by his unconscious. The moment the patient begins to withhold from the analyst, consciously, information of *any* kind, he sets an additional barrier between himself and his "cure."

The patient must eventually be able to know the facts about himself. He must also be able to accept these revelations without any sense of fear or shame. What may seem to him the most trivial or irrelevant of facts may really be of deep significance. The fullest possible story about himself is the only way to the fullest possible analysis.

A patient who withholds information from his analyst is not much different from a man with stomach trouble who refuses to tell his symptoms to his family doctor.

**Are the patient's personal revelations kept secret?**

Yes.

The confidences of the patient in analysis are treated with the same discretion as are those of the lawyer's office and the priest's confessional. They are offered for the ears of the analyst alone, and by tradition they go no further.

The Hippocratic oath, formulated some twenty-four hundred years ago, is still accepted by physicians as an article of faith. It includes a line which recognizes the need for complete confidence between doctor and patient: "Whatsover in my practice . . . I shall see or hear amid the lives of men I will not divulge, as reckoning that all such things should be kept secret. . . ."

Every qualified psychoanalyst abides by this oath.

**Is treatment by two analysts better than by one?**

No.

There are no doubt good reasons, at times, for having two lawyers or even two physicians handling a single case. In analysis, however, the peculiar nature of the patient-analyst relationship makes such an arrangement unwise. Instead of speeding up treatment, it would be likely, only too inevitably, to slow it down. As a result, much of the benefit a man or woman might otherwise derive from treatment would probably be cancelled out.

A patient who imagines that an additional analyst might bring him additional benefit is probably not anxious to make progress. Without realizing the fact himself, he is resisting help rather than seeking it. Unconsciously, his real aim is to play off one analyst against the other. With two analysts, his allegiance would be divided. He would then find it easier to resist acceptance of what he learns about himself from either one of the analysts. His treatment would therefore be unnecessarily prolonged, and the date of any eventual "cure" would be pushed farther and farther into the future.

No qualified psychoanalyst is likely to treat a patient who is being treated at the same time by another analyst.

### Is a patient "cured" when he knows the facts about himself?

No.

It is not enough for the patient, consciously, to know the facts about himself. He knows, of course, that this represents a long step forward. But this step, as long as it may be, is only a first one. The patient must develop more than just an understanding of the neurotic forces which dominate his behavior. He must learn of the constructive forces within himself as well. And even this is far from enough. To achieve success in analysis, much more has to be done. And the real difficulty comes with trying to make progress against the resistance of the unconscious part of the mind.

Acquiring knowledge about oneself usually implies some need for change. But the unconscious will not change without a long and bitter struggle. This struggle uses up vast quantities of time and energy on the part of both the patient and the analyst.

The struggle is not ended until the unconscious has finally yielded to the conscious. That happens when the unconscious, too, "knows" and accepts the facts. Only then is the analysis complete.

### What determines the end of a patient's analysis?

The analysis is over when the patient realizes that his conscious mind, rather than his emotions, is now in command of his way of life. (See above.) This does not have to be pointed out to him by the analyst, since it is something he is able to feel clearly in himself. He knows this feeling in a variety of ways. He is now free, for instance, from the particular neurotic symptoms which originally brought him to the analyst.

He now feels "good" about himself, and this feeling is evident in almost everything he does. His job, for instance, is no longer a source of irritation or boredom for him; he gets a sense of satisfaction from it. He actually enjoys the things he does for pleasure, instead of merely going through the motions of enjoying them. The disappointments or even the defeats of the day no longer throw him off balance. He is now able to take his troubles in stride.

As for the other people in his world, they have ceased to present special problems to him. He gets along with them quite well. He respects their needs and interests as he now looks to them to respect his own. And he is now better able to be open and direct in expressing his feelings of love, as well as better able to accept love from others.

When a person has been successfully analyzed, he is able to face the demands of life without evasion. He makes his own decisions. Far better able, now, to use his maximum abilities, he is in a position to mold his environment wherever possible, and adjust to it wherever necessary.

Life, he knows, means problems, but he is now prepared to deal with those problems.

### What is group therapy?

Group therapy is a comparatively new technique for treating emotional problems.

The group feeling is a strong one among human beings, and the need for kinship finds expression in all branches of our society. It shows itself in what we call "team spirit," a feeling appealed to frequently in such activities as athletics, business and warfare, for instance. We see other evidences of this feeling in the formation of get-together organizations. Fraternal groups such as the Masons or the Knights of Columbus, even women's clubs and the Boy Scouts, are based largely on the deeply human need to join hands with our fellows in some fashion.

The group feeling is, in fact, not much different from a kind of family feeling. It makes most people aware of being just a bit less alone in the world. In group therapy, this powerful human urge to "belong" is used as a weapon in the fight against neurosis.

Psychoanalysis has learned that certain types of patients are now able to solve their problems faster when working coöperatively with other patients. For them, progress is faster as a member of a group than when closeted alone with the analyst.

It is this same principle, incidentally, which helps the members of such a group as Alcoholics Anonymous to make successful war on their problem. Isolated from others, the alcoholic usually faces a far more difficult struggle in trying to conquer his illness.

In group therapy, the analyst may be able to treat anywhere from six to ten patients during the same session. In addition to other advantages, the cost to the patient, per session, is less than for individual treatment.

As a technique for the treatment of certain kinds of emotional illness, group therapy is a rapidly expanding phenomenon. More and more therapists are learning to use it every year.

### What takes place in a group therapy session?

Six to ten patients, sometimes all men or all women but more frequently a mixed group, meet regularly, usually one evening per week, in the presence of the analyst. There, seated comfortably about a room, they spend an average of an hour and a half in discussion of their separate problems.

There is no formality about the procedure, and it bears some resemblance to a "bull-session." The only obligation is to speak the truth. A patient may talk about himself, about those around him, or even about people or situations outside the room. But in any case, he must try to express frankly the thoughts closest to himself. His fears, desires, dreams and preoccupations of the moment become topics for group discussion. He may be interrupted at random by any of the others present, with comments on what he is saying.

A newcomer is usually startled by the depth and range of personal revelation at such a session. It is as if he were expected to tell, to a friend of one day, the confidences he might hesitate to offer after a few years. But the group therapy situation accelerates a sense of openness on the part of the individual. In a short time the newcomer may find himself joining the discussion freely with the others. He rapidly loses his sense of self-conscious restraint. In the course of only a few sessions, he is likely to become an actively contributing member of his group.

Under the supervision of an analyst, group therapy gives the patient the opportunity to talk about his problems in a kind of social situation. He is able to speak with complete freedom to a number of his fellows who can help him to achieve personal understanding and insight.

**How does group therapy work?**

A patient in group therapy examines his problems face to face with half a dozen or so other people. All of these other patients have problems similar to his own.

He faces also, in a way, a replica of the family situation he knew as a child. In his childhood, chances are, he contended with brothers and sisters for the attentions of a parent. In the group, the analyst affects the feelings of the patient in the same way that a particular parent once did. And the other people in the group affect him in the same way as the brothers and sisters with whom he competed in his earliest years.

To the patient, the group is also like a miniature of

society. It is, as the saying goes, a "reasonable facsimile" of the world outside the room in which the sessions take place. Although each of its members is to some extent neurotic, the sum total of all the members, with their individual differences, their separate virtues as well as their problems, is equal to one solidly "normal" point of view. It is this normal point of view of the group which helps each of the members forward to improved mental health.

Whether he wants to or not, the patient reacts continually to those around him in the group. In many situations there, he re-lives the feelings which moved him when he was a child. These are the same feelings which show themselves in his attitudes toward life and the world in which he lives.

Little by little, the patient's real self is exposed not only to the group, but also to himself. Some of it is made plain by analysis of his dreams and some through discussion of his problems. And there is likely to be additional revelation for him in the way he addresses himself to the problems of other members of the group. It is through the examination of his reactions to these others that he achieves the greatest understanding of his own problems. And each member of the group, in learning more about those around him, learns more about himself.

In time, in the group atmosphere of acceptance plus mutual insight, the patient's problems may be resolved.

### Who practices group therapy?

In this country today, there are more than a thousand specialists in the practice of group psychotherapy. Of this number, only two out of every five have a medical degree, and of these, not all are actually psychoanalysts. Some are psychiatrists who have been influenced by analytic techniques.

The largest number of practitioners (three out of five) includes lay analysts, psychologists, ministers and social workers, among other kinds of psychotherapists.

### What is the cost of group therapy?

Group therapy is less expensive to the patient than individual analysis (see page 93). According to a recent survey, more than two-thirds of the men and women receiving this kind of treatment pay fees of between five and ten dollars per session. Twenty percent of the remainder pay five dollars or less. And in some situations, the fee for each session is reported as being only fifty cents.

### Is group therapy a substitute for psychoanalysis?

No. But it can be an auxiliary tool.

Group therapy cannot be a substitute for psychoanalysis because it cannot probe as deeply into the patient's mind. But it provides an analyst with a more direct means of attack on certain specific types of emotional problems. These problems are usually related to how the patient gets along with other people. They are of a type that may be more expediently handled in a group than through individual treatment.

A psychoanalyst who practices group therapy is likely to see his individual patients privately in addition to meeting with them in the group. But there are patients, of course, who are able to profit from group therapy alone.

### What is psychosomatic medicine?

The word "psychosomatic" comes from two Greek words which mean "mind" and "body." This branch of medicine is concerned with discovering the ways in which a sick mind may affect a healthy body, and a sick body may influence a sound mind. While the word "psychosomatic" may be new, the idea behind it is not. It can be traced back at least to Aulus Cornelius Celsus, a Roman medical historian of some two thousand years ago. He recommended that any physician who sought to cure his patient should get to know the patient's mind as well as his body.

Psychosomatic medicine takes as its basic premise a single important fact: In every human being, the emotions and the body are continually acting upon each other. Anger, for instance, can give us a headache, and excitement can cause us to perspire. And a sickness or accident can cause us to feel depressed, irritable, sorry for ourselves, or to suffer some state equally emotional.

There is no such thing as an ailment that is purely emotional or purely physical. An emotional difficulty will always affect a person's physical well-being in some degree, no matter how slight, and the reverse of this is just as true.

In a sense, practically every family doctor has had some experience in the practice of psychosomatic medicine, whether he calls it by that name or not. For example: spring fever, deep anxiety, or even being head over heels in love, can produce physical symptoms. And there is always the patient who just wants a little attention. When the family doctor faces such symptoms, he is usually able to prescribe for them on the basis of his common sense, if not his experience. He has probably met them often enough before.

Up to recent years, when a man showed some symptom of physical illness (aches, pains, digestive disturbances, paralysis, etc.) he would be treated for a physical condition alone. In many cases, this physical condition would remain, despite the best efforts of the doctor. In other cases it might disappear under treatment, only to be replaced by another symptom or ailment, which would have to be treated in turn.

The results of psychosomatic research show that, often enough, physical ills can be cured only by some form of psychotherapy.

*For example:* A young woman, the sole support of her

mother and father, gives up the idea of marrying the man she loves. She makes this decision because she feels that her parents need her. Suddenly she develops severe backaches. Examination by her doctor reveals nothing physically wrong with her back. But the attacks continue. An expert in psychosomatic medicine would, in such a case, try to help the girl find the underlying emotional reason for her illness. When this reason was discovered and dealt with, her physical symptom would, in all likelihood, disappear.

Although this branch of medicine is a comparatively new one (in terms of serious study), it has made tremendous strides. In a relatively short time it has opened up a new approach to the treatment of ailments which had formerly been considered entirely physical.

Psychosomatic medicine is a major concern of psychoanalysis.

**Is one's physical condition often affected by one's emotions?**

Yes.

Most people are familiar with conditions such as "nervous stomach" or the headache that comes from "just nerves." These are everyday examples of the ways in which emotional strain can affect a person's physical condition.

The National Association for Mental Health has estimated that half of all the people who come before the family doctor are suffering from some kind of mental or emotional illness. Some psychoanalysts have placed the figure even higher. To them, seven out of every ten patients visiting the doctor have ailments which are the result of some emotional problem.

There is no way to check the accuracy of such estimates. But experience has shown that a wide variety of afflictions, normally considered entirely physical in nature, can often be cured by some kind of psychotherapy.

Some of the ills which may be produced or aggravated by emotional distress: asthma, ulcer, ailments of the digestive system, heart trouble, menstrual difficulties, muscular tics, backache, stammering, skin trouble, some forms of paralysis, and even some blindness. The complete list of such ailments is far too long to be set down here.

## What Psychoanalysis Can and Cannot Do

### What does an analysis aim to do?

SIGMUND FREUD COMPARED psychoanalysis to the working out of a jigsaw puzzle. The object is to make a single, unified picture out of a jumble of separate fragments. There can be only one solution, and until it is achieved no clear picture is possible.

Most people lack this clear picture of themselves. With them, the unconscious mind remains a hodgepodge of elements which deeply affect the character of each such person. Because this jumbled image has never been assembled into clear focus, the lives of most of us are only half lived in terms of what they might be.

When a patient first comes to analysis, he usually knows only the most superficial facts about himself. He remembers easily enough the more obvious points in his personal history. But even though he is conscious of certain dissatisfactions with the way in which he has been living, he does not understand the real reasons for these dissatisfactions. The underlying causes of his fears, his frustrations and his failures are a complete mystery to him.

A man may be afraid of responsibility, impatient with his children, or continually angry with his wife. In each of these cases he may convince himself that he knows exactly the reason why he reacts as he does. Despite this self-assurance, however, the real reasons are beyond him.

It is the work of analysis to educate the patient to understand the *why* of his own particular feelings and behavior. To do this, the unconscious portion of the mind must be systematically explored. When this has been accomplished, the patient may begin to shape, for the better, his attitudes and his life. All of life is a kind of struggle, and a successful psychoanalysis is expected to equip a person for that struggle.

When psychoanalysis has been successful in piecing together the jigsaw elements of the inner picture, the result is a person who is aware of his own real feelings and abilities. He is able to accept them, to act upon them, and to enjoy them. In plain language, he is able to face life not as an overage infant, but as an adult.

### Is psychoanalysis a "last resort"?

In a way, yes.

Most people, when in trouble, prefer their remedies to be quick, inexpensive, and as simple as possible. But of all forms of treatment for emotional problems, psychoanalysis makes the greatest demands on the patient. It takes the greatest amount of time; it is the most expensive; and it subjects the patient to the severest personal ordeal.

For these reasons, psychoanalysis is often the "last resort" of the man or woman who needs help.

### Does analysis make one's personality bland and colorless?

No.

A successful analysis eliminates only the unhealthy elements in the patient's personality. The urge to dominate or impress others by superior use of words, ideas, humor, or even gestures, is a neurotic one. Anyone who uses one or more of these techniques as a social weapon is usually expressing a symptom of some emotional problem. Under analysis, such a person would not lose any of his natural capacity to be entertaining or even brilliant. None of the basically valuable elements in his personality, in fact, would be tampered with. But his use of these capacities would be altered.

For one thing, his talents would no longer serve the needs of his neurosis. He would no longer be witty or brilliant at the expense of others. All his positive social qualities would continue to function, but now they would do so without the taint of neurosis. Any native capacity he may have to express himself intelligently or interestingly would now be able to show itself more attractively and less hurtfully than before.

Many actors, actresses and entertainers have been psychoanalyzed, with no noticeable decline in their "personality." Also, it might be pointed out that psychoanalysts, as a group, do not suffer the reputation of being bland and colorless. Yet every psychoanalyst has been through analysis as a patient.

### Does analysis teach the patient to adjust to "the worst"?

No.

Psychoanalysis teaches the patient to cope with his environment at the best possible level for himself. It does not educate him to accept the status quo merely because it exists.

Every patient is expected to learn how to change the conditions around himself for the better within the bounds of possibility. This may mean showing him the way to a better job; it may show him the way to get along better with the people who come into his life; it may bring home to him an awareness of his responsibilities as a citizen living in a community. He learns, generally, to become a better person. And he also learns to become a more active one.

There is no accepted form of psychoanalysis which teaches a person merely to tolerate his difficulties.

### Does psychoanalysis make one an "average" person?

No.

The so-called average person is one whose life, ordinarily, is victimized by emotional forces within himself—

forces of which he is only faintly aware, if he is aware of them at all.

It is the aim of psychoanalysis to help the patient to work his way out of this "average" condition. It does this by making it possible for him to remove the various unconscious factors which have blocked the fullest development of his life. And where these factors cannot be completely removed, the patient learns at least to understand them and to contend with them intelligently.

When a man has been successfully analyzed, he is usually able to think more clearly (and more often) than most of the people around him. He can also act more decisively, and generally can make better use of what life and his own abilities have to offer. Such a man's attitude toward life and toward himself will, in fact, be considerably different from the average.

### Does a successful analysis increase one's will power?

Yes.

Psychoanalysis, to be considered successful, must equip the individual with command over himself. This control is a more comprehensive form of what we usually mean by the term will power.

Will power is nothing more than the ability to say Yes or No, as the case may be, and act as if we mean it. Many a man, for instance, thinks he deserves a raise at the office. He would like to ask for it, but is afraid to do so. He may even soothe himself with all sorts of reasons which indicate the wisdom of not asking for the raise "at the present time." Such a man cannot, somehow, say a wholehearted Yes to what he considers a legitimate demand.

Many people, too, have been in situations in which a superior whom they dislike extends to them an invitation of some kind. They would like nothing better than to say No, but they cannot bring themselves to do so. They imagine all sorts of unpleasant consequences, should they express what are actually their true feelings in such a situation.

Perhaps even more familiar is the situation in which no one but oneself is involved. If we are overweight and ought to go on a diet, we more than likely reassure ourselves that we will do so "soon," or "next week." If we smoke too much, and know that we ought to cut down, or even give up the habit entirely, we can usually manage to postpone doing so "for a while, anyway."

A person who has been successfully analyzed is able to say Yes and No, and mean it.

**Does psychoanalysis make one a nicer person?**

As a rule, yes.

When a man cannot get along with other people, there is usually a sound reason for it. His emotions, operating from a neurotic basis, have colored his behavior and his thinking.

Such a man may have a malicious tongue. He may be annoyingly selfish or even miserly. He may be aggressively noisy or even downright cruel. In any of a dozen other antisocial ways, he may be a poor risk for friendship (or even decent relations) with others. All of these quirks are symptoms of inner emotional pressures.

Psychoanalysis reduces these pressures in the individual. By educating him to understand what it is in himself that makes him tick, it makes him the master rather than the slave of his own emotions. It gives him a sense of emotional security, and this relieves him of the need to soothe any inner tensions at the expense of the people around him. The result of such changes is usually a socially "good" person.

There are many people, however, who are considered to be "nice" only because they tend to agree with just about everybody, and about almost everything. They seem never to say No. Such people are usually afraid to come to grips with life by facing situations honestly. They sense that the man who agrees with everyone will move through life, as a rule, with a minimum of outward trouble. People are bound to like someone who never disagrees with them, the reasoning goes. But the inner cost of such an attitude is usually very great.

Successful analysis enables a person to stand up for his own rights. Let us suppose that this person had not been in the habit of standing up for these rights. Then, this newly-won ability to prevent his being "pushed around" may cause him to be considered no longer a "nice" person. But this opinion is likely to be held only by those who formerly were able to profit, in one way or another, from his earlier timidity.

**Does psychoanalysis make one more intelligent?**

No.

It does not affect the basic intelligence of the patient, either for better or for worse. But it can remove many emotional stumbling blocks which formerly prevented the best possible use of the patient's mental powers. It thus makes for a more active and effective use of his native intelligence.

Among other things, and more important perhaps, it enables the patient to reason more clearly in problems directly affecting himself. And when this happens, he is able to act more intelligently.

**Can a successful analysis perform "miracles"?**

No.

Every major benefit in the course of psychoanalysis is achieved only through the patient's will to coöperate with the analyst. This means work. It is not enough for the patient simply to understand the basic causes of his feelings and behavior. He must be willing, by his actions, to make his knowledge a part of his conscious life.

Psychoanalysis is not much different, in this sense, from other forms of education. What a person learns from it is only one part of the benefit. What he does with what he learns is even more important. And in both the learning and the doing, the patient is very much on his own.

Psychoanalysis can offer no miracle drug or automatic results. The active effort of the patient is required before any benefit can be achieved. Shakespeare offers a glimpse of this same idea in one of the closing scenes of *Macbeth*. After many crimes, Lady Macbeth has suffered what we might call a nervous breakdown, the result of her feelings of guilt. After the doctor returns from her bedside, Macbeth asks:

How does your patient, doctor?
DOCTOR: Not so sick, my lord,
As she is troubled with thick-coming fancies,
That keep her from her rest.
MACBETH: Cure her of that:
Canst thou not minister to a mind diseas'd,
Pluck from the memory a rooted sorrow,
Raze out the written troubles of the brain,
And with some sweet oblivious antidote
Cleanse the stuff'd bosom of that perilous stuff
Which weighs upon the heart?
DOCTOR: Therein the patient
Must minister to himself.

That doctor did not practice psychoanalysis. But if he had, he would have still found it necessary to emphasize the patient's need to help herself.

People who see such man-made marvels as Boulder Dam for the first time are inclined to regard it as a "miracle" of modern engineering. Any modern engineer knows, however, that far from being a miracle, it is the product of hard work.

## Does an analyzed person have problems?

Yes.

To live in this world is to have problems. But an analyzed person understands himself in relation to his problems. He is therefore able to cope with them. Such a person is unlikely to be upset *unnecessarily* by any difficulties which life may present to him.

As with anyone else, it is entirely possible for an analyzed person to be fired from a job, injured in an accident, or suffer the loss of a loved one. But he has trained himself to be able to take such problems, when they touch him, without being reduced to a state of collapse. Because of this, his problems have little chance to dominate his thinking and actions to the degree they might if he had not been analyzed.

As for problems which originate within oneself, an analyzed person continues to have those, too. He may have to contend with a tendency to impatience with others, excessive self-centeredness, an inclination to shyness, or to other hangovers from his life before analysis. But his understanding of these problems in himself will usually temper their expression. Also when other people have been made to suffer through his expression of these problems, he will know how best to remedy the situation.

Civilization has been described as a problem-breeding organism. The aches and pains of a complex society cannot be affected by psychoanalysis. But the man or woman who must live in such a society is able to do a far better job of it after having been analyzed successfully.

## Will analysis increase one's earning power?

As a rule, yes.

A man in need of psychoanalysis is not able to use fully all the talents with which he is endowed. This is often reflected in his pay check, which may not correspond to what he should be earning on the basis of his real abilities. Psychoanalysis teaches him to make the most of these abilities.

*For example:* A fairly common type is the man (or woman) who is satisfied to bury his talents in some relatively unrewarding job. This job does little to challenge his real abilities, and the pay, only too logically, is correspondingly low. Many talented people, unaware of their capacities, tend to waste their abilities in this kind of situation.

In the course of analysis, a patient with such a problem may discover why it is that he seeks to bury his abilities like this. And he may in time be able to do something about it. For the mature person, one's gifts are more than a privilege. They are a responsibility.

On a more obvious level, there are many people who are simply incapable of asking a boss for more money, a landlord for more steam, or a grocer to take his hand off the scale. One of the major goals of any successful analysis is the improvement of the patient's sense of self-esteem. When this is achieved, he is better able to ask for (and get) what he thinks he deserves.

For the average patient, one of the earliest results of progress in treatment may be an increase in earning power.

**Does analysis ever act as a crutch?**

Yes.

People who require some kind of crutch in life are likely to seize upon almost anything: money, religion, drink, drugs, and certain kinds of political belief, among other possibilities. Psychoanalysis, too, is sometimes seized upon as a crutch. An occasional patient will hang on desperately to his emotional troubles, blinding himself to any path out of his personal jungle. His unconscious resistance to the benefits of analysis can be very great.

Such a patient resists making an end to his problems, because he cannot face the prospect of putting an end to his analysis. Unconsciously, he is unable to give up the comfort and understanding he has found in his relationship with the analyst. It reproduces for him his childhood relationship with his father or mother.

Just as that patient was once afraid to grow up because it meant leaving the comfort of his home and parent, so he is now afraid to grow up emotionally and leave the analyst. He is afraid to take his place in life as a healthy, independent human being.

An analyst can usually recognize, soon enough, the patient who uses his treatment as a crutch. Once recognized, this problem, like others, is explored. In time, it becomes possible to bring such a patient around to a more constructive attitude toward his treatment. Whether the time this takes will be longer or shorter will depend on the skill of the analyst and the resistance of the patient.

### Is analysis a threat to the creative person?

The ability to create something out of one's imagination is a positive, socially valuable asset, and psychoanalysis claims to help rather than hinder the use of this asset.

Underlying every work of art is some measure of creative ability, and a particular neurosis may cause this creative energy to be expressed in a specific way. Analysis does not affect this basic creative talent. But it seeks to break down the neurotic barrier which may stand in the way of the greatest development of that talent.

Edgar Allan Poe, Toulouse-Lautrec and Richard Wagner were all eminent men in their separate arts, and they were all quite neurotic. But psychoanalysts contend that these men were great not because of neurosis, but in spite of it. Had it been possible for each of these men to be analyzed, they suggest, each would perhaps have learned to express his art from a different personal point of view.

And if such were the case, there is no reason to believe that any of them would be less famous than he is today. In addition, all three would have been less embattled human beings. They might have led happier lives.

On a lesser level than the trio mentioned, there are many thousands of genuinely creative persons who produce nothing at all. A poet has commented that the world is deprived of more art through lack of character than through lack of talent. The victims of this problem of character are prevented by neurosis from making any attempt at all to display their real talents. They turn their backs completely on their possibilities as creative persons.

There are a great number, also, who make only a kind of left-handed use of their artistic talents. These are the ones who somehow get trapped in kinds of creative expression which are really only a compromise, or dead end, for their abilities. A potential poet, for instance, may spend his life writing advertising copy. A serious artist may find himself designing textiles. And someone of deep musical talent may find himself teaching music appreciation rather than composing music to be appreciated.

In such men and women, neurosis has diverted genuine talent off the main highway and onto a detour. And with such as these, psychoanalysis is often a long step in the direction of that main road. It can prepare the way for the development of such a patient as a truly creative person.

It is not the "wrong" things in a person's makeup that result in art, but the "right" ones. And psychoanalysis concerns itself with eliminating only the "wrong" elements in the personality of the patient.

**Can analysis break up a marriage?**

Yes.

It is not unusual to hear of a marriage that has been broken as a result of the husband's or wife's having been in analysis. But when this happens, it is usually because the basis for the marriage was faulty to begin with.

Psychoanalysts maintain that such a marriage would probably have collapsed, in time, under any circumstances. They do not necessarily mean that the two people would inevitably have been divorced. But what they do mean is that any feelings of warmth, or attraction, that might have been originally responsible for the marriage, would cease to exist sooner or later.

Many persons marry the wrong partner for the wrong reasons. Our high divorce rate (one divorce for every four marriages) is one indication of this. Social scientists agree that the rate would be even higher were it not for certain preventive factors. Many unhappily married couples, for instance, give up the idea of divorce for reasons of religion, because they have children, or even because they lack the money to go through with it. Marriages are not destroyed by analysis, it has been pointed out, but by husbands and wives.

To any fundamentally sound marriage, psychoanalysis is likely to add something important. This something is a measure of real understanding, the greatest possible insurance of permanence in any relationship. The patient gains insight into himself and others which helps him to cherish the solid virtues in his marriage. He is able to take a less impatient view of those frictions which might put his marriage, in other circumstances, under a strain.

As a rule, psychoanalysis tends to be a conservative influence on a marriage. Its views may seem to be, to some, even old-fashioned. It does not, for instance, condone adultery as a form of "hygiene" guaranteed to keep a marriage from falling apart.

**Does psychoanalysis make a person happy?**

No.

Ordinarily, what we call happiness is determined by

two sets of factors: One set is internal, and the other is external. Analysis can make a human being *able* to be happy, but it can do nothing about the world in which he lives. If his environment is depressing and he can do nothing about it, then he is unlikely to be happy. But he will be able to adjust to these unhappy circumstances with more ease and less pain than will the person with emotional problems.

When circumstances permit, the analyzed person is able, better than most, to experience those joys that the world around him has to offer.

If it were possible for any one person to be happy all the time, he would have to be some kind of mental case. Happiness is, to borrow the words of the popular song, "a sometime thing." The man who has been analyzed is likely to be receptive to that "sometime" when it presents itself. He has graduated from that large class of people who seem to refuse, even under the most pleasant circumstances, to be happy.

**Is analysis a threat to the religious person?**

If a person is truly religious, no.

There are many reasons which may bring someone to belief in religion, but these reasons are not always necessarily good ones. History shows many cases of leaders, for instance, who used belief in God—or even a special way of believing in a special god—as a means of advancing their own personal ends.

Lesser persons may use religion for lesser goals.

*For example:* A man may use religion as a means of relieving himself of the responsibility to be ethical, since he is able to convince himself that his faith will bring forgiveness for sin. He has only to believe, and to go to his church, and he feels relieved of any need to be truly "good."

There are some people who use their religion as a kind of social weapon. It permits them to feel superior to other people who do not happen to share their religious beliefs.

For many people, religion is a kind of special soothing syrup. It provides them with a needed sense of being watched over, because they are too weak to face the harsh circumstances of life without this kind of support.

These are only a few of the less worthy reasons for being "religious." Such men and women, as a result of analysis, may learn the true reasons why they lean on something which is for them only a crutch. Through this understanding, the need for religion merely as a form of moral first aid is lessened. With clearer mind, a belief in God may then be approached on a level which is far more intimate and personal. And this firmer belief can be less self-seeking because it can be essentially more self-giving.

For those who already approach God with a sense of selflessness, psychoanalysis can only fortify their inner awareness of faith. This inner strength of belief is part of the same human resource which analysis itself must exploit in order to bring about its best results. Real religion, and psychoanalysis, draw their power from the same dynamo in the individual—a basic sense of what it means to be really "good." Ultimately, they aim also to produce the same kind of person: One who is responsible, honest, and at peace with himself (and with others).

Sigmund Freud, it is true, regarded religion as primarily a product of neurosis. Children, he pointed out, tend to feel helpless. They yearn for the protection of a father. In the same way, he believed, man seeks, through religion, the protection of the most powerful of all fathers. From this point of view, religion is an attempt on the part of the individual to gain some control over a world which contains many conditions and situations which are threatening to him. In its own way, Freud's view of the origin of religion was not too distant from the often-quoted remark of Voltaire: If God did not exist, then man would have to invent him.

But despite Freud's own opinion, many psychoanalysts have chosen to differ with him on religion, and are themselves religious-minded men and women.

Also, there are today many ministers and rabbis who have been specially trained to provide pastoral counseling to the members of their congregations. This training, as a rule, is influenced by the Freudian approach to psychotherapy.

Another indication of the relationship between psychoanalysis and religion today: At the world-famed psychoanalytic institute, the Menninger Clinic, at Topeka, Kansas, Roman Catholic priests have, on occasion, participated in seminars. Also, the Union Theological Seminary, one of the largest Protestant seminaries in the country, carries on a program aimed at illuminating the links between religion and psychiatry. Since its inception, this program has been directed by a psychoanalyst.

### Does psychoanalysis see man as basically "good" or "evil"?

It was the opinion of Freud that every man and woman has the capacity to be both good and bad. We are, he felt, mixtures of the two. And each of us has it within himself to be not only better than he thinks he is, but also worse. For every Hitler there is a Gandhi, and for every Torquemada there is a St. Francis. And in the average man or woman, these opposing tendencies exist side by side.

This view of each man's capacity to be both very "good" and very "bad" is not really original with Freud. As he himself was well aware, it had been noticed by many before him.

*For example:* "Good and evil we know in the field of this world grow up together almost inseparably; and the knowledge of good is . . . involved and interwoven with the knowledge of evil, and in . . . many cunning resemblances hardly to be discerned. . . ." That was written by John Milton, more than three hundred years ago.

A common-sense view of this same condition was offered by Samuel Johnson, little more than a hundred years after Milton: "As it is said of the greatest liar that he tells more truth than falsehood, so it may be said of the worst man that he does more good than evil." To this there are of course exceptions, as there are to any general rule. But where these exceptions exist, they are likely to do so in those rare cases of people with disordered minds —psychotics, fanatics, and others who have lost touch with reality.

For most people, the general view of psychoanalysis on this particular problem is contained in the words of the old rhyme:

> There is so much good in the worst of us,
> And so much bad in the best of us,
> That it ill behooves the most of us
> To find any fault with the rest of us.

**Does analysis free the patient from all moral restraint?**

No.

By common definition, a moral person is one who conforms to the rules of right conduct. Anyone who has been successfully analyzed fits well within the meaning of this definition. He is able to distinguish between right and wrong, and to act accordingly.

It is true that psychoanalysis tries to rid the patient of many of his inhibitions or repressions. These are the internal strains which have kept him from his fullest possible development as a human being. But when these inner distortions are corrected, his attitude toward morality remains unimpaired. It may in fact be improved. A tendency to easy morality may have been one of the symptoms of his neurosis.

*For example:* At the end of his analysis, a man may be able to cut down drastically on a tendency to excessive drinking, gambling, or the undiscriminating pursuit of women. These may have been—and usually are—ways in which deep inner tensions have sought to express themselves.

It is primarily one's attitude to oneself that is affected by analysis. A person may lose a false sense of guilt, or feelings of general anxiety. He may no longer suffer from a constant sense of being inferior to other people. He may free himself of anything from insomnia to an inability to have a satisfactory sexual relationship with the woman he loves. In none of these cases, or similar ones, is his sense of what is "right" likely to be deteriorated.

Precisely because he has managed to build in himself a sound core of inner strength, he is better able to lead a truly moral life. Because of his acquired understanding, an analyzed person is usually able to do the right thing even when it hurts.

**Does psychoanalysis encourage sexual promiscuity?**

No. (See above.)

This is a common misconception of the function of psychoanalysis.

The urge to be sexually promiscuous, when it is discovered in a patient, is treated as a neurotic problem. No psychoanalyst is likely to encourage a patient to acquire such a problem. Where such a tendency already exists, the analyst will almost certainly see that it is analyzed.

**Does psychoanalysis ever fail?**

Yes.

Every idea which has ever been developed for the purpose of helping human beings has had its quota of failures. Along with medicine, marriage and religion, for instance, psychoanalysis too has its share of lost hopes.

Among the failures of psychoanalysis are a large number of men and women who did not persist in treatment. Somewhere this side of successful analysis, they found some convenient excuse for cutting their therapy short.

Some of the reasons most frequently offered at such times are:

"I can't afford it any longer."

"I'm getting nowhere."

"It's taking too long."

"Things are happening too fast. I need a little time off, just to get my bearings."

"I know enough about myself now, I'm sure. I can go the rest of the way on my own."

Any one of the reasons the patient offers to the analyst (and to himself) in such a situation is likely to seem only too plausible. But the real reason, not quite so apparent, is in each case the same. It is the patient's unconscious resistance to the inner changes imposed by a successful analysis. In terms of warfare, it is like a final, massive rear guard action, in which all reserves are thrust desperately into the struggle. It is a last stand.

Many animals are gifted by nature with some particular mechanism for self-preservation. The deer can outrun its enemies, while the lion is stronger than the beasts it contends with. The chameleon can use protective coloration, the skunk its peculiar smell, and the porcupine its shield of needles. The 'possum is able to fool many of its enemies simply by playing dead. The human animal, of course, has many different methods of protecting himself. Not the least of these is the ingenuity with which he is able to fight off, unconsciously, the need for deep inner change. (See page 91.) It is this that may try, when all else fails, to persuade the patient that, for one reason or another, he must put a stop to his analysis.

As a rule, the analyst is able to convince the patient of the real reason for his decision. But this is not always possible. Some patients develop such a strong resistance to further treatment that they desire to end it no matter how transparent their excuses may be made to seem. The flimsiest excuse will sometimes suffice, and the direst warnings of the analyst may go unheeded. Such a patient feels that it is less painful to him to live with his problems than to probe any deeper inside himself.

A man or woman who has left analysis under such conditions has, of course, been "in analysis." Such a person's unexamined emotional problems will continue to produce symptoms. When these are noticed by other people who are unaware of all the facts, it is not unusual for the blame to be put on analysis.

Psychoanalysis has its share of honest failures. Most of them, again, derive from the patient's resistance. But in these cases, the patient willingly persists in treatment. At some point, however, with certain patients, the march into the interior of the mind comes up against an inner wall on which is painted, in effect, "They shall not pass." When this obstacle is reached, treatment can go no farther.

When progress is blocked in this way very early in analysis, the treatment may be considered a failure. When it is blocked later, after noticeable benefit to the patient, it may be termed a partial failure (or perhaps a partial success). In both types of cases, when the time comes that no further help can be afforded the patient despite his conscious wishes, he is discharged.

It is not possible for psychoanalysis to perform miracles. Like every other branch of reality, it is subject to certain limitations.

*For example:* Suppose you are seated in a crowded bus. Another passenger, stepping past you, manages to crush your toe under his heel. If it is an obvious accident, you will be likely to excuse an action that was, at worst, due only to clumsiness.

Now suppose, in that same bus, the other passenger crunched down on your extended toe out of sheer deliberate malice. Your reaction then would be less forgiving. Angry words might be provoked, perhaps even a fight. At the very least, you would have strong feelings of resentment.

So much for your attitude, which in the two cases would be distinctly different. But despite this difference, the toe would be in exactly the same condition in either case: it would hurt. And it is even possible, despite the best medical attention, that it may be damaged in such a way as to trouble you for the rest of your life.

So it is with a wound which is felt in a person's unconscious. Under psychoanalysis, it is possible to explore the reasons for the wound. But psychoanalysis can work no magic. It is sometimes impossible to heal that inner wound to the point where the personality is "as good as new." But by understanding the nature of his hurt, the patient is better able to live with it.

Finally, not all psychoanalysts are equally competent at solving all types of problems. (See page 76.) It is always possible for the wrong analyst to be treating the wrong patient. This is a risk which is run by anyone with special problems who seeks the counsel of a doctor, a lawyer, a dentist, or any other type of professional consultant.

**Is psychoanalysis only for mentally unsound people?**

No.

Psychoanalysis is not able to do very much for the

psychotic. It can be of no help to the man or woman who suffers from a really severe mental disorder. It can offer its benefits only to those who are able to lead ostensibly "normal" lives. But these people have two things in common: They are dissatisfied with the lives they lead, and have an active desire to do something about it.

*For example:* A man may feel dissatisfied because of an ever-present sense of personal failure. He knows that he should really be able to do better in life than he has been doing, but he feels powerless to change matters.

Another man may seem unable to fall in love, although he is sure he would really like to. Meanwhile, all his friends have become married, and yet for all his effort, no woman seems able to win his devotion.

A third man may have everything that most of us understand by the word "success." He has an attractive wife and family, a good job, many friends and a respectable position in the community. And yet he seems incapable of enjoying any of this. Life is an ordeal for him, and he does not know why.

A man (or woman) may feel a sense of personal dissatisfaction for any of these reasons, or for many more. And once the feeling takes hold, it tends to feed on most of the situations in which that person finds himself. Such feelings have no respect for individuals. Men and women in all walks of life, holding positions on all levels of responsibility, may suffer from them.

It is to people such as these that psychoanalysis can offer help.

**Can a person's wealth reduce his need for analysis?**

No.

With material wealth, a man can solve only his material problems. It is just as easy for a rich man to feel dissatisfied with himself as it is for a poor one. The ability to live with oneself, and with others, on the best possible level, has no relation to one's financial standing.

Wealth can provide a man with attention, but not necessarily with respect. It can surround him with pleasant people, but it has no special value in helping him to make real friends. It can make beautiful women readily accessible to him, but it cannot guarantee love. And when a rich man is alone with himself, his money can provide no real immunity against self-doubt, anxiety or dissatisfaction. The suicide rate among the wealthy, for instance, is not as low as some people might suspect.

Money is no adequate armor against emotional troubles. But it can, of course, make treatment for those troubles readily available.

**Can children be psychoanalyzed?**

Yes.

There are analysts who specialize in the treatment of children. Emotional pressures have little respect for the innocence of youth, and children are subject to them at least as readily as are their elders. In recent years, the psychoanalysis of children, either individually or through group psychotherapy, has expanded. Their emotional difficulties, it has been found, lend themselves to this kind of treatment.

When such therapy is brought to bear on the problems of the young, it is likely to head off problems which may, if untreated, require far more attention in years to come.

**Does psychoanalysis advise that children should be permitted to do "everything"?**

In the opinion of Freud, repression of one's wishes and desires plays a major role in producing neurosis. But it was never his idea that in order to prevent neurosis, children should be permitted to do anything they feel like doing.

Prohibitions of some kind are a necessary element in educating any child to grow up in a world of other people. If it were possible to permit a child to grow up in an atmosphere of absolute personal freedom, it would almost without a doubt develop serious emotional problems. Quite possibly, by the time such a child became an adult it would be regarded by its fellows as some kind of a monster.

In order for any child to reach real maturity as a social being, some kind of prohibition, or discipline, must be provided. It is in the administering of these disciplines—the when and how of them—that trouble may arise.

**Must the patient believe completely in psychoanalysis in order to benefit from it?**

No.

If this were true, it has been pointed out by analysts, then it would be impossible for children to be treated with any effectiveness.

Many people come to analysis with reservations about certain of its theories. Sometimes such reservations are based on misinformation. In such cases, the patient's own experience in treatment will usually dispel these misgivings.

At other times, some neurotic need of the patient makes it necessary for him to withhold complete confidence from the analyst. When this happens, appropriate doubts are usually forthcoming. There may be other reasons, as well, to cause a man or woman to doubt the validity (or just some aspect) of psychoanalysis.

But when there are doubts in the patient's mind, and when they stand in the path of therapy, they are treated like most of his other doubts: They are analyzed.

**Is the patient helped more easily when he is well-read in psychoanalysis?**

No. The opposite is probably closer to the truth.

When a patient enters analysis after having read a great

deal on the subject, he may well present special problems to the analyst. Such a patient's ordinary resistance to the progress of therapy (see page 91) may be reinforced by what he has read.

*For example:* During his sessions, he may set himself up as a kind of competitor of the analyst. He may do this by having his own ideas about exactly how therapy should proceed. And of course he will advance his own ideas at every opportunity.

He might also "discuss" his problems on the basis of what he has read, instead of talking spontaneously about them. His reading may encourage him to intellectualize his feelings. In a way, he is able to hold these feelings out at arm's length from himself, and discuss them as if they were not really his own.

The well-read patient is equipped at all times to throw an especially intricate roadblock into the path of analysis. Such a patient is able to lend to his resistance a very powerful tool. All resistance to therapy is time-consuming, and the patient's ability to quote chapter and verse often makes it more difficult to get down to the bedrock of his problems.

**How many people in this country have been analyzed?**

There is no central source from which any accurate answer to this question could come. For this reason, any statement of the number of Americans who have been psychoanalyzed would be only the roughest kind of guess. But there can be little doubt that the total is quite low. The comparatively small number of psychoanalysts in this country (see page 75) has been a major reason why this kind of therapy has been limited to the few.

In 1956, *Time* magazine advanced the following estimate: "Perhaps 15,000 patients are in analysis at any one time; the estimated total of Americans who have tried analysis (though many did not stay the full course) is well over 100,000—more than in the rest of the world."

It must be remembered that this figure of "over 100,-000" would represent the total of all Americans who have had some contact with psychoanalysis during a period of about half a century.

## Paths Away from Freud

**Do all psychoanalysts agree on principles?**

No.

All accredited analysts admit a tremendous debt to Sigmund Freud as the founder of psychoanalysis and the man who formulated its basic theories. Not all analysts, however, give equal value to the specific theories advanced by him.

By far the largest number of analysts in this country may be considered Freudian. Some of them are "orthodox" in that they hold firmly to all the principles of the founder.

A small number of others are "eclectic." The dictionary defines this word as "choosing from various sources," which is just what this kind of psychoanalyst does. As a general rule, the eclectic analyst takes most of his ideas from Freud. But he also incorporates into his approach those ideas advanced by other contributors to the field which are in his opinion worthwhile.

There are other "schools" in addition, none of which boasts a particularly large group of practitioners. Analysts affiliated with these schools tend to accept fewer of Freud's beliefs than do the members of the orthodox or even the eclectic groups. These schools may accept some of Freud's beliefs only in part, and substitute theories of their own for others.

The American Psychoanalytic Association, the dominant professional body in the field, is a Freudian organization. It is the largest single psychoanalytic group in this country.

**What are the principal non-Freudian schools?**

There are five leading schools of psychoanalysis which differ strongly enough with Freudian beliefs, on some points, to have charted forms of therapy distinctly their own. These five groups are made up of the followers of Alfred Adler, Carl Jung, Otto Rank, Karen Horney and Harry Stack Sullivan.

Each of these five founded a small but active school of analysts which subscribes to his theories and practices. Although all five of these originators are now dead, their schools are functioning today.

**What are the beliefs of the Alfred Adler school?**

Alfred Adler (1870-1937) was an early pupil of Freud. In 1912, he broke away from his teacher and founded his own school, offering his theories under the name of "Individual Psychology."

He believed that it was man's search for power, and not his sexual drives, that determined the way he thought, felt and acted. To Adler, this seeking after power or dominance was the single most important factor in the life of any man or woman.

It was Adler who invented the term "inferiority complex." Every man and woman has some feelings of inferiority, he believed, and out of these feelings comes the need to feel superior to those around us.

*For example:* Before Demosthenes became the greatest orator of Greece, he had been a stammerer. Napoleon, who was short in stature, became a great general. The poet Byron, his physical appearance marred by a deformed foot, made a good part of Europe a playground for his love affairs. Each of these men, according to Adler's theory, "compensated" in his own way to make up for his physical handicap.

In the same way, Adler argued, people tend to compensate for emotional difficulties as well. Take a man who has a deep feeling of personal unworthiness; this lack of self-esteem may drive him to become dictator of his country, or governor of his state, or just the top man in his office. In any case, it may drive him to achieve some position of superior eminence. He would thus be proving to himself, perhaps, that others were even lower than himself.

Other persons, for not so obvious reasons, may be led into nursing, into writing, into having many children, or into some other activity. They choose these particular lines of effort simply as a means of compensating for an emotional injury of which they are unlikely to be consciously aware. In Adler's opinion, these drives, depending on their strength and their direction, determine for each of us whether we will be successful or unsuccessful, mature or neurotic.

In Adler's view, our society tends to put the male on a sort of pedestal, making him a symbol of strength and leadership. The female, in contrast, is a symbol of inferiority and weakness. This he believed to be responsible for many emotional problems, not all of them peculiar to women alone.

Freud thought that it was important to search the past, to examine the roots of the patient's neurosis. Only in that way, he felt, could its causes be discovered. But Adler disagreed. He believed that a person's goals play a major role in making him neurotic. He was therefore more interested in studying the patient's aims, in trying to discover what he was trying to get out of life. False values, plus the psychic effort necessary to keep such values in operation, could have a disastrous effect on the individual, according to Adler.

An analysis by a follower of Adler tends to concern itself with the day-to-day problems of the patient. Also, it is likely to take a shorter time than would a Freudian analysis.

**What are the beliefs of the Carl Jung school?**

Carl G. Jung (1875-1961), like Alfred Adler, was an early pupil of Sigmund Freud. Also like Adler, he broke away from his teacher at the beginning of this century. Jung founded what in time became a new approach to psychoanalysis. He gave it the name "Analytic Psychology."

Jung believed that the patient has little chance of achieving a successful analysis until he is past middle life. In his view, psychoanalysis is best suited to the patient who is already thirty-five or over, although in recent years this figure has been lowered considerably. Also, the Jungian patient is not usually considered "cured" until he has developed a personal sense of religion which is both emotionally and intellectually satisfying to him.

It was Jung who first pointed out the importance of the parents' influence in the life of the child. It is the atmosphere they provide, he said, that directs the child either toward maturity or toward neurosis. Also, he wrote, it is the parents' influence which determines the particular kind of neurosis from which the individual may suffer. This theory, like some of the others which he advanced, has become part of the generally accepted body of psychoanalytic knowledge.

In his writings, Jung noted that each of us carries within himself memories of more than merely his own experiences. We carry as well, deep inside ourselves, memories that originated far back among our remote ancestors. He called this legacy of the past the "collective unconscious." It is a grab-bag of ancient memories which we all share. Its existence is proved, he maintained, by the fact that widely separated peoples, in different parts of the world, have often been found to make use of the same kinds of myths, symbols and rituals.

This theory of Jung's is viewed with respect by most analysts. Those outside his own school, however, do not give it the emphasis, in the course of treatment, which his own approach to the patient seems to demand.

Today, in fact, the differences between Freud and Jung show up far more clearly in the treatment of the patient than they do in the theory alone.

In Jungian analysis, the will of the analyst plays a more prominent role than it does in other schools of psychoanalysis. In this form of therapy, for instance, the analyst's relationship to his patient is almost that of a teacher to his pupil. Opponents of Jung's views believe that this offers the patient less opportunity to develop a personal sense of will and a real capacity for making his own decisions.

Analysis by this method usually takes more time than does any other form of psychoanalytic treatment.

### What are the beliefs of the Otto Rank school?

Otto Rank (1884-1939) was a third pupil of Freud to break away and found his own school.

According to Rank's theories, all people tend to fall into three general classes:

First is the normal or adjusted person. He accepts the ideas, the standards and demands of the world about him. He believes that these ideas, standards and demands are completely in accord with his own way of life. Because he believes this, he is able to go about the business of living with a minimum amount of friction.

Second is the neurotic person. Not only is he unable to adapt himself to the popular will, but he also lacks the strength to stand up solidly for his own ideas. As a matter of fact, according to Rank, the inability of such a person to conform may, through emphasizing his aloneness, provoke in him a feeling of guilt. This adds additional weight to his neurotic burden.

Third is the creative artist. In Rank's view, a truly creative person is able to accept himself completely. He is able to fuse his abilities and ideas into an expression of himself which the world calls art. He thus becomes a positive individual, on a somewhat elite level. According to Rank, such a person stands beyond the need for any kind of treatment.

Rank felt that it was the aim of all treatment to make the patient able to assert himself. He must be educated to express his own sense of will, rather than to ape the wishes and ideas of those around him.

The emphasis, in this type of psychoanalysis, is on the situations of the present, rather than those of the past. This is so, despite the fact that the central theme of Rank's theories is the tremendous shock suffered by each of us as a result of the simple act of being born. The single moment when the individual is separated from his mother and thrust into the world is the "birth-trauma" (the shock of birth).

According to Rank, this particular instant, when each of us is thrust away from his mother for the first time, is the most deeply significant in the life history of any individual. It produces a vast fund of tension in every man and woman, and this enormous burden on each of us is eased only bit by bit in the course of a lifetime. In neurotics, this load of anxiety never really diminishes at all.

Psychoanalysis by Rank's approach is likely to take a shorter time than by the Freudian method.

### What are the beliefs of the Karen Horney school?

The theories of Karen Horney (1885-1952) are, on several counts, reminiscent of Alfred Adler's. There is, for instance, the same emphasis on the importance of the goals a person sets for himself in life. Each of these analysts makes the same point: False values lead to false goals, and false goals lead, in turn, to neurosis.

According to Horney, the more unreal a man's image of himself and what he wants out of life, the more likely he is to have emotional problems. As an analyst, she examined at length the effects of various kinds of social pressures on the life and attitudes of the average man. Competition is one example of these pressures. Freud, she felt, had largely underestimated the importance of these forces in shaping people's emotional lives.

Like Adler, Karen Horney considered the social elements in a person's life to be more important than the sexual elements in determining the nature of his neurosis.

In the course of treatment, the followers of Horney place the greatest emphasis on the patient's difficulties of the moment. His current problems—what is happening to him *now*—and the part which his neurosis plays in these problems, are considered of primary importance. Much less importance is attached to the past life of the patient.

A psychoanalysis conducted by the Horney method takes approximately the same amount of time as by the Freudian method.

**What are the beliefs of the Harry Stack Sullivan school?**

Harry Stack Sullivan (1892-1949), American-born, introduced into psychoanalysis the theory of "Interpersonal Relations."

This theory is based on the belief that the personality of each one of us is molded from birth by the people and the social forces met with in our environment. Sullivan's followers are usually termed members of the "Washington School," since it was in this nation's capital that the founder and his colleagues did much of their early work.

There are two major human desires, according to Sullivan. The first is biological. It concerns itself only with our bodily needs, and it seeks constant satisfaction. The second drive is largely social. It is aimed at achieving, for each of us, a sense of personal security in the society in which we live.

Sullivan believed that in every person there is, from his beginnings, an urge to gain the approval of those around him. Hand in hand with this is an urge to avoid disapproval. Together, these twin pressures play a central role in shaping a person's life. They have much to do with determining how he will live his life.

Unlike Freud, Sullivan put great stress on the capacity of the environment and social pressures to shape the life of each of us. The way a person behaves in the present, he believed, can best be explained by examining his current "interpersonal relations."

What happened to a patient in the faraway past is of considerably less importance, in Sullivan's view, than what is happening to him at the moment. In this respect, his beliefs closely resemble those of Adler and Horney.

The patient's cure, according to Sullivan, can be accomplished only by the gradual unfolding of the real meaning behind his relationships with other people.

A patient being analyzed by this method will usually spend about the same amount of time as he might in a Freudian analysis.

**Are there other schools that differ with Freud?**

Yes.

There are well over two dozen separate "splinter groups" at odds in some measure with Freudian beliefs. Each of these groups bases its differences with Freud on some individual approach to treating the patient. These differences with orthodox analysis may be, as in some cases they are, only minimal. In other groups, the differences with Freudian belief may be just about total. Most such schools tend to have a bare handful of practitioners. In some cases the "school" may be limited to the person who founded it.

Among these lesser groups, it is possible to find a great many separate and distinct approaches to the treatment of the individual's emotional problems.

*Some of them:*

orgone therapy
rational therapy
conditioned reflex therapy
directive therapy
non-directive therapy
family therapy

This, of course, represents only a small sample of available forms of therapy that deviate from Freudian principles. There are many others.

## Emotional Problems and the Average Man

**Does the normal person differ sharply from the neurotic?**

NOT NECESSARILY.

The so-called "normal" person has normal emotional mechanisms. The neurotic has these same mechanisms, but in him they operate in an exaggerated form.

*For example:* A normal person has an understandable interest in his own health and safety. He sees his doctor when necessary, is careful crossing streets, and if he drives a car, does not make a practice of exceeding the speed limit. His attitude toward life and its problems is likely to be a reasonable one. There may be situations in which he will suffer from some degree of anxiety: a shake-up at the office will mean that some jobs will have to be eliminated, and perhaps one of them will be his own; a loved one is very ill; he is having trouble with his landlord, who threatens to have him evicted. In any of these sample situations, a normal person's worries would be in some reasonable proportion to what may *probably* happen. His imagination will not tend to give excess color to the dreadful possibilities.

A neurotic person, in contrast, may have an abnormal interest in his own personal health and safety. He may be a hypochondriac who spends much of his time at the doctor's office. He may look to crossing the street as a dangerous ordeal and take elaborate precautions before doing so. And he may never drive a car at all, because he fears a possible accident. Unlike the normal person, the attitude of the neurotic toward life and its problems tends to be more an emotional than a reasonable one. And he is likely to worry about a situation in terms not of what is *probable,* but what is *possible.*

As with a physical ailment, such as an infection or a toothache, for instance, emotional illness may be acute or it may be chronic. Many people who are neurotic do not call attention obviously to their emotional difficulties. Their deviations from the norm may be trivial, or perhaps may simply go unnoticed by others. But whether they are obvious or only dimly sensed, the symptoms are there. And, as in the case of infection or toothache, when neurosis persists and is untreated, it is likely to get worse.

**Does a neurotic person always know he is neurotic?**

No.

When a man is neurotic, he is often the last person to realize that there is anything wrong with him. His need to feel that he is perfectly all right may be so great that he cannot really be objective about himself.

Even though his world—his family situation, his job, his relations with his friends—may be falling about his ears, he may be totally unaware that something in himself is at fault. It is usually easier for him to blame his misfortunes on his neighbors, his boss, "the breaks," the system, or even his friends and loved ones. Any reason may serve, as long as it permits him to shift the blame from himself.

In a way, the neurotic is like a man who is colorblind and does not realize it. Confusing red with green, he has a great deal of trouble with traffic lights. Sometimes, in fact, his distorted vision may get him involved in very serious situations. When this happens, such a man thinks he is being quite logical in blaming his situation on someone or something outside himself.

**Does a neurotic person affect other people?**

Yes.

This is especially true when the neurotic is in a position of authority. As a boss, he will find ways to gain satisfaction at the expense of his subordinates. As a parent, his neurosis will have a harmful effect on his relations with his child.

As a friend, a husband, a lover, or even a fellow employee, the problems of the neurotic are bound to affect the way he gets along with other people. And as an ordinary human being moving about in the world, his neurosis will leave its mark on his associations with those people with whom he comes into contact.

Since every relationship is influenced to some extent by each person in it, the neurotic affects the lives and feelings of all persons around him. The closer his tie to someone, the more likely it is that his emotional problems will affect that person.

### Is it "wrong" to be neurotic?

Many people react to the word "neurotic" as if it were a label signifying something morally "wrong." But there is as little reason for attaching social stigma to neurosis as to defective eyesight.

Neurosis is as widespread in our society as the common headache. (See below.) When a man suffers from headaches to such a degree that they impair his everyday way of life, he usually goes to a doctor.

In a society where mere living is as complicated as it is in ours, everyone is neurotic to some degree. As with a headache, the greater the degree of neurotic illness in an individual, the greater his need for some kind of professional help.

### How widespread are emotional problems?

Almost everyone comes face to face with emotional problems in the course of a lifetime. In trying to solve these problems, each of us meets with varying degrees of success.

It has been estimated that one person in every ten suffers from some kind of serious emotional disturbance at some time during his life. At least as frequent is the emotional problem of someone close to us.

Perhaps there is an alcoholic in the family. Or there may be a husband, a cousin or a friend who just can't seem to hold a job, although he appears to be bright enough and willing enough. Or there is, often enough, the attractive young couple whose marriage is going to pieces for reasons no one seems especially sure of. All of these are emotional problems for the persons directly involved. In addition, they send out vibrations of a sort which affect emotionally the persons who come in close contact with those directly suffering from these problems.

There are countless other men and women who walk through life bothered with vague feelings of uneasiness and dissatisfaction. They may use some word less serious than "problem" to describe this feeling, but whatever they call it, it is a problem to them nevertheless. It keeps them from living the kind of life they are basically fitted for and would really prefer to lead.

Three out of every ten persons, it has been estimated, spend their lives below their own best level of personal well-being and efficiency. This is a direct result of some emotional difficulty. It means that in the United States there may be as many as fifty million men and women who lead lives which lack a real sense of fulfillment.

Here are some other figures, recorded or estimated, which help to give some idea of the spread of emotional problems in this country:

1) According to the opinion of experts, there are in America today more than five million "problem drinkers."

2) Some sixty thousand Americans are believed to be regular users of narcotics.

3) At current rates, one marriage out of every four

finds its way into the divorce courts. Unrecorded are the many marriages which remain intact only because divorce is out of the question for some reason—religion, lack of money, children, etc.

4) Official records show that some eighteen thousand men and women succeed in committing suicide every year. But, for one reason or another, a great many self-inflicted deaths are not recorded as suicide. The real figure, therefore, is probably substantially higher than the official one. Also, the number of people who attempt to destroy themselves, and fail, is very great.

All these figures represent human beings with problems. Most of these men and women could probably be helped by some form of psychotherapy.

### What did our ancestors do about their emotional problems?

Our forebears did not understand the real nature of their emotional problems, and therefore did little about them. Many sought relief in religion, from the family physician, or by confiding in friends. And great numbers, of course, suffered in silence.

Today, life is a far more complex experience than it was in the days of our ancestors. Consequently, the pressures on the emotional life of the average man and woman are much greater. Even our way of describing these pressures has changed. Long ago, for instance, people would speak of having "troubles," a word of almost homely simplicity. It is only in comparatively recent times that people began to use a more ominous word; they began to speak of having "problems."

The majority of people with "troubles" or "problems" continue to rely on the methods of their ancestors in seeking relief for their emotional ailments.

It is interesting to compare people's attitudes toward

their emotional problems with the way they feel about their physical problems. The men and women of long ago faced severe hazards in trying to maintain their general health. Often they lived in hopelessly unsanitary conditions and were subject to widespread epidemics of disease. This was usually the result of mere ignorance. They received inferior (if any) medical treatment for their physical ills. And they lived much shorter lives, as a rule.

Since then, there have been striking advances in general medicine, and most people have been willing and even anxious to benefit from these advances. But despite equally impressive advances in psychological medicine, the public has lagged far behind in its acceptance of these developments.

**Can a neurosis be conquered by will power alone?**

No.

Will power, no matter how forceful, is unable to do the job alone. It is possible for a strong-willed person to do away with a particular symptom of neurosis, but that is all.

It is not impossible for a man who is neurotic to abolish an habitual eye twitch, the chain-smoking habit, or a compulsion to count every traffic light he passes in his car. But the neurotic basis of the particular symptom would remain. And as long as the neurosis itself continued untouched, another symptom, perhaps of a different type, would soon appear. The new symptom would then have to be contended with.

In addition to an effort of will, some kind of valid treatment is necessary before one can hope to remedy a neurotic condition.

**Does it help to be ignorant of one's emotional problems?**

No.

According to the proverb, ignorance is bliss, but only

where it is folly to be wise. The underlying emotions of a man make up the single most important element in determining his feelings, his actions and, in essence, his life. It is a fundamental belief of psychoanalysis that this is one area in which what a man doesn't know *can* hurt him.

People accept the fact that it is best to discover a disease of the body at the earliest possible moment. The more promptly it is found out, the sooner the treatment can begin and the more likely it is to be successful.

Speed in beginning treatment is equally important in dealing with emotional problems. Unfortunately, many people with such problems do not understand that anything is wrong with them. Large numbers of others may realize that they have problems, but do not feel they have any particular need for treatment.

A man who is unaware that he is neurotic is affected by his neurosis despite his unawareness. Day by day, subtly or obviously, it influences the way he feels, the way he thinks and the way he behaves. When things go wrong, there are always plausible excuses for him to offer. He can blame it on luck, on some other person, or on practically anything else that may seem reasonable to him.

But, as with a disease of the body, ignorance only permits the condition to flourish.

**Is it wise to keep emotional problems to oneself?**

No.

Personal secrecy about one's emotional problems, far from relieving them, is likely to increase their pressure. Most men and women are familiar with perhaps the oldest and most widespread form of release for inner tension —discussion of a personal problem with a sympathetic and intelligent listener. In psychoanalysis, as in other types of psychotherapy, this kind of discussion serves as a primary means of reducing emotional pressure.

On its most elementary level, the mere fact of speaking out about one's feelings can act as a safety valve. In this connection, the English poet, William Blake, wrote a poem more than a century ago, which he called "The Poison Tree." The first stanza contains some very good advice about the value of speaking out:

> I was angry with my friend:
> I told my wrath, my wrath did end.
> I was angry with my foe:
> I told it not, my wrath did grow.

**Can emotional problems be inherited?**

No.

Unlike physical characteristics, a parent's emotional problems cannot be passed along to a child by heredity alone. After the child is born, however, it will certainly be affected by the atmosphere in which it lives. And its parents have a great deal to do with the nature of that atmosphere.

A baby is an extremely sensitive instrument. It reacts emphatically to the subtlest discords in its immediate environment. It is a major tenet of psychoanalysis that early childhood is the most important single period in the development of one's personality. An infant is totally dependent on the world around it, and can easily be made to feel defenseless, abandoned and unwanted.

When a child feels its world to be hostile to it, the child becomes hostile to that world. And when either or both of the parents of a child have emotional problems, the child is likely to develop similar emotional problems of its own.

*For example:* A mother is abnormally preoccupied with the idea of financial security for her family. This expresses itself in a variety of ways. She nags her husband to get a better job; she constantly looks for new ways to cut corners in her expenses, and is very "saving" in matters of food, clothes and transportation, as well as other areas; and she often denies the family opportunities for pleasure because "money doesn't grow on trees."

This excessive emphasis on the importance of money is communicated to the child. As a result, it grows up with a distorted view of the value of money in the individual's life. Other values, which may be of greater importance, are shunted aside. The child may then carry into adult life, like a germ, the mother's besetting interest in financial security.

### What is a nervous breakdown?

A nervous breakdown is, actually, the breaking down of an individual's ability to control himself. The phrase refers to any condition in which a person's nerves or emotions are so disturbed that he is no longer sure of what he is doing.

In a way, such a person loses contact with the world in which he lives. His condition may last for only a few weeks, or it may drag on for years. When someone has a nervous breakdown, however, the results are always the same. There is a deterioration in his relations with the people around him. His ability to carry on with his work is impaired. And he has difficulty, in fact, in getting on with the ordinary business of living.

A nervous breakdown usually requires some kind of professional attention. In extreme cases, where severe mental illness has set in, it is often necessary to place the victim in an institution until he has recovered.

### Where can a poor man get treatment for emotional problems?

In larger cities, it is often possible to get some kind of low-cost psychotherapy at one or more of the local hospitals. It is also possible, in some areas, to receive this kind of aid at clinics maintained by private institutions or groups. A phone call or letter directed to the county medical society, the local mental health society, or the nearest hospital, will ordinarily provide information as to where such low-cost treatment is available.

Psychoanalysis is not available through any public institution. Its costs, over the necessarily long period of treatment, tend to put it out of the reach of those on the lowest economic levels. But it is possible for even these people to provide themselves with therapy—through facilities indicated above—which is oriented along psychoanalytic lines.

### Is mental illness common?

Yes.

When people have emotional problems, they may continue to lead their normal lives while under treatment. People who must be treated for mental *illness,* however, are as a rule removed from their normal lives. They are usually taken care of in hospitals, sanatoriums, or other institutions.

Victims of mental illness occupy approximately half of all the hospital beds in the entire United States. More people suffer from this kind of sickness than from cancer, heart disease and infantile paralysis combined. It is America's number one health problem.

Not all people who suffer from mental illness are in institutions, however. Great numbers of them walk the streets, trying to lead normal lives without benefit of treatment. Such men and women carry their problems with them into every situation that touches their existence.

### Can mental illness be prevented?

Mental illness is often the direct result of some physical breakdown. Possible causes include hardening of the arteries, syphilis, encephalitis, or cerebral palsy. A person who has come down with one of these diseases may suffer damage to his brain. When this happens, he becomes the victim of a mental illness which usually requires professional attention.

Many of the patients in mental hospitals today are there as a result of some kind of physical breakdown. It is possible that their mental illness could have been prevented only insofar as their original physical illness could have been held in check.

Other patients in such institutions are there for reasons which have no traceable physical cause. With many of these, mental illness has acted like a delayed-action bomb. The fuse was lit in childhood and set to explode sometime in later life. This bomb, in the form of a breakdown, usually blows up in the mind of the individual, often in reaction to some immediate situation. And when it does blow up, it usually brings personal disaster in its wake.

Until the blow-up, a man may seem perfectly normal to his friends and neighbors. Then one day he does something dramatic or violent (or both) which lands him in the hospital psychiatric ward, if not in jail.

If the symptoms of such a person had been recognized early enough, either by himself or by someone competent to judge them, suitable treatment might have been started. This early treatment might have arrested or perhaps even cured the condition. This latter kind of mental breakdown —the result of the individual's personal reaction to the world in which he lives—can usually be prevented.

### How does a person know when he needs help?

When a man breaks an arm, he goes to a doctor. When he needs money in an emergency, he usually borrows from a friend or from a bank. When he is hungry, he manages somehow to get food. Each of these situations is one in which the individual takes care of some immediate and personal need.

The particular signal indicating the need for emotional help is rarely so obvious. And it may vary from person to person. Generally, however, it shows itself in an ever-present sense of personal dissatisfaction.

This may take the form of a feeling that things never seem to go right. It may mean the inability to get enjoyment from anything, whether a relationship, a job, or even one's pleasures. It may come from an oppressive and continuing sense of failure as a human being, whether in relation to circumstances or to other people.

Basically, however, it shows itself in a conscious and chronic feeling of dissatisfaction with oneself. When a man is able to admit to this feeling, he is ready to see some kind of psychotherapist.

**Can emotional pressures be relieved by amateur help?**

Yes.

Talking to a friendly, intelligent and sympathetic person can often provide superficial relief for one's tensions. This is especially true when these tensions are the result of anger, fear, or frustration, for example.

**Can amateur help cure one's emotional problems?**

No.

Very often, in fact, amateur help can be dangerous. There is a widespread interest in psychoanalysis, and great amounts of literature on the subject are everywhere available. This has equipped society with an army of volunteer "psychoanalysts" who are only too anxious to assist others in solving their emotional problems.

Analysis is a long-term process requiring maximum skill, knowledge and objectivity on the part of the analyst. It is unlikely that a friend who is willing to help solve one's problems will be able to fulfill the specifications.

Emotional problems can be serious problems. The advice of an unqualified friend or acquaintance will not cure them. Even though administered with all the good will and seeming authority in the world, such advice may have disastrous results.

In many fields, no great harm is done by assuming that "an expert is anyone who knows more than I do." But the treatment of emotional illness is a job for professionals only.

**Is there prejudice against psychoanalysis?**

Yes.

The general public is at best dimly aware that such a thing as psychoanalysis exists. Among those who are familiar enough with the term to have formed an opinion about it, there is often prejudice against it.

**What causes prejudice against psychoanalysis?**

Psychoanalysis is a comparatively new development in the field of medicine. Like other developments which were once new and even revolutionary, it has had to fight, during its beginnings, against a considerable amount of resistance.

The first men to introduce vaccination, the use of chloroform, or even procedures of simple cleanliness in operations, met with similar antagonism. General medicine has been practiced for a very long time, and as of today it has just about won its war as far as public opinion is concerned. When people object to it nowadays, their objections are likely to be expressed in marginal terms. They may for instance object to fees, or the practices of some individual doctor, or perhaps even to the attitudes of doctors as a group. But they are unlikely to question the value of medicine itself.

Where analysis is concerned, the attack is very often wholesale, with little sympathy shown for any aspect of it. Much of the prejudice against it is based on misinformation as to what it is and what it aims to do. While this obstacle has faced new developments in almost every field, psychoanalysts can point to a number of additional reasons why Freud's theories find no easy acceptance:

1

To many people, sex is a highly inflammatory word. Such people strongly resent the idea of psychoanalysis. It intrudes into an area they feel is not only highly personal, but enveloped (and rightly so, they believe) in taboo. Such people can feel easily threatened by the idea that "psychoanalysis is only interested in sex."

2

When Copernicus wrote that the sun, and not the earth, is at the center of our universe, people roundly condemned the idea. It robbed them of their sense of importance in the scheme of things. Much later, Darwin wrote that man was not descended from Adam and Eve through some deliberate act of God. As a matter of fact, he wrote, there were some depressingly inhuman ancestors in man's family tree. People were very much angered by that idea, too. They felt that it deprived them of their special relationship with God.

When Freud came along with the idea of psychoanalysis, most people were again disturbed. He was telling them, in effect, that they are unable to govern their own lives. Something deep inside them, which he chose to call "the unconscious," was the secret director of the average man's life.

It is not hard to understand why a great many people might resent the idea that they do not really control their own thoughts, feelings and behavior.

3

Psychoanalysis seeks, through what seem to be unorthodox methods, to alter the individual's way of life. This makes it especially subject to emotional attack.

Every person tends to feel afraid when his own way of life, the way in which he gets along with himself and with the world, is threatened.

Every one of us, in order to reach some measure of bearable adjustment with life, must make some sort of compromise. Each of us arranges this compromise behind his own back, so to speak. It is not done consciously, in such a way that we are really aware of it. Here is how it happens:

In every man and woman, the unconscious mind makes certain demands for satisfaction. Many of these demands must be denied because something in us recognizes them as being unlawful, unethical, or generally irresponsible. Each of us, then, must stifle (or at best disguise) those of our yearnings which we feel would be unacceptable to those around us.

This enforced censorship is the price each of us pays for living in a civilized society.

*For example:* An aggressive man might feel like murdering someone who has offended him. This would mean his trial and possible execution. But he may disguise his hatred in the form of sarcasm. Or he may hide his aggressiveness behind a generally pessimistic view of everything and everyone around him. When he covers his feelings like this, the world will at least tolerate them.

In the same way, a man with strong sexual feelings knows that he cannot force his attentions on any woman he desires. Society has ways of punishing that kind of behavior. Such a man, then, may become merely a "wolf."

Also, the man who values money above everything else could yield to his feelings and rob a bank. But he may choose a less violent alternative and become a highly successful, but ruthless, business man.

The second course of action in each of these examples represents a compromise between basic unconscious drives and what the world will allow us to do. To a greater or lesser degree, practically all persons make some such bargain between their secret selves and the demands of living. This bargain does not guarantee them happiness, but at least it permits a measure of getting on in the world.

When the status of this bargain, this way of life, is threatened, the inner man becomes panicky. Psychoanalysis implies change in the individual, and it is primarily in the area where each of us has made his bargain that this change must occur. It is this fact which offers so much of a threat to those anxious to hold on to their own kind of compromise.

Ralph Waldo Emerson, who lived many years before psychoanalysis, observed, "We are afraid of truth, afraid of fortune, afraid of death, and afraid of each other." Psychoanalysis, more than any other kind of psychotherapy, tries to make the individual face all his fears and all the truths about himself. It is for this reason more than any other, psychoanalysts believe, that it provokes prejudice or even resentment among many people.

## For Further Reading

ALEXANDER, Franz, *Fundamentals of Psychoanalysis.* New York, W. W. Norton & Co., 1948.

ENGLISH, O. S., and PEARSON, G. H. J., *Emotional Problems of Living.* New York, W. W. Norton & Co., 1955.

FREUD, Sigmund, *A General Introduction to Psychoanalysis.* New York, Garden City Publishing Co., 1943.

HEALY, William, BRONNER, A. F., and BOWERS, A. M., *The Structure and Meaning of Psychoanalysis.* New York, Alfred A. Knopf, 1930.

HENDRICK, Ives, *Facts And Theories of Psychoanalysis.* New York, Alfred A. Knopf, 1946.

KUBIE, Lawrence S., *Practical and Theoretical Aspects of Psychoanalysis.* New York, International Universities Press, 1950.

MENNINGER, Karl, *Love against Hate.* New York, Harcourt, Brace & Co., 1942.